D1015677

GOIN' TO THE CHAPEL

GOIN'
TO THE
CHAPEL

Dreams of Love,
Realities of Marriage

CHARLOTTE MAYERSON

BasicBooks
A Division of HarperCollins*Publishers*

Designed by Laura Lindgren

Library of Congress Cataloging-in-Publication Data

Mayerson, Charlotte, 1927–
  Goin' to the chapel : dreams of love, realities of marriage / Charlotte Mayerson.
     p.   cm.
  Includes index.
  ISBN 0-465-04180-9
  1. Marriage—United States.   2. Married women—United States—Psychology.   I. Title.
HQ734.M4414   1996   96-20146
306.81—dc20   CIP

96 97 98 99 00 ❖/HC 10 9 8 7 6 5 4 3 2 1

To my pals, Anne and John Zinsser

CONTENTS

ACKNOWLEDGMENTS

The organizations and individuals who helped me find the participants in this project were astonishingly cooperative and helpful. Though I can't mention their names, I can say how grateful I am to them. As to the women across the country who spoke to me about their lives, they were generous with their time and with the insights into their own marriages they shared with me. Without them, obviously, this book would not exist. Without them, my own life would be a lot poorer.

I am very lucky in my friends. They have the virtues of generosity, humor, and loyalty. They are also very smart and—however you judge this quality—very picky. If this book is less than they hoped for, it is probably because, in certain instances, I was too stubborn to do what they told me to.

First, to three great editors, representing three generations of splendid and meticulous craftswomen, I want to express my loving thanks for the time they took, the intelligence they dispensed, and the good humor that prevailed. Who else has these qualities in such large measure but Genevieve Young, Wendy Sanford, and Caroline Sutton?

I thank also these other wise readers and specialists: Paula Doress-Worters and Judy Norsigian of the Boston Women's Health Book Collective; social psychologist Miriam Ehrenberg; psychotherapist David Eidenberg; anthropologist Shirley Gorenstein; scientist Joyce Margolis; social thinker Michael Phillips; psychotherapist Susan Robertson; and publisher Wellington Watters.

My agent, Anne Sibbald, of Janklow & Nesbit Associates, has been an efficient, kind, and ever-available support. Charles Levine saw the potential of this project when it was still only slightly more than a gleam in my eye. At Basic Books, my editor, Editorial Director Susan Rabiner, helped me carve a book out of a weighty tome. Her responsiveness has been enormously important to me. Associate Publisher Gay Salisbury's infectious and informed enthusiasm for the book was very important, as was the knowledge and energy of publicist Susan Furst. Susan H. Llewellyn was a sharp-eyed copy editor and Karen Klein an enormously sensible production editor. Juliana Nocker expertly and cheerfully complied with my requests for all sorts of help. To all of them, my gratitude.

Charlotte Mayerson
December 1995

‒‒ I ‒‒

THE UNDERLYING QUESTIONS

t seems a little juvenile to begin a book with the story of what I did on my summer vacation but it was a trip I took in 1990 that launched me on this journey into the dreams and realities of marriage. I had just come through a bad period in my own life, a time when you want to protest to the authorities: "This isn't what I had in mind." To catch my breath and make a start at reorienting myself, I took time out and headed west, where I allowed the weather, the terrain, and a fat address book to idly tumble me, like a rolling stone, from Seattle down to Los Angeles.

The analogy doesn't quite work. Stones tend to be pretty quiet; I, on the other hand, spent those months gabbing—engaging in a lot of intense talk with the people I ran into and with the friends I visited along the way. Mostly it was women I was conversing with and, I soon realized, mostly it was marriage we were chewing over . . . when we married, whether we'd divorced, what we'd expected beforehand, what we'd come out with.

For example, in a tiny ranch town in southeastern Washington, I made an admiring comment to the woman spooning out my lamb stew about a good-looking man of a certain age who'd just paid his bill. Lillian, who owned the restaurant, giggled and told me she'd been in love with him for the full four years of high school. She then ticked off all the reasons he'd have made a hopeless father to her children. We sat exchanging confessions until, at about seven-fifteen, she turned the sign on the door CLOSED side out. "Nobody eats much later around here," she said, "and there's nothing left in the pot anyway."

During my travels I began to notice that a certain phrase kept coming up: "Well, it isn't what I expected but . . ." Sometimes the woman would go on to say that her life is different but better than what she anticipated; sometimes the words triggered a special sadness, as somebody set her real marriage against what she had envisioned for herself when she was a girl. And I suspect that the phrase was particularly evocative for me, at a time when my own life was so far from what my girlhood dreams had prepared me for.

I started to write down what I was hearing, first as a sort of travel diary, then because I came to appreciate how moving, funny, and stimulating the conversations were. By the following winter, back in New York where I live, I understood that, beyond their personal interest, my notes raised issues about marriage that had not quite been addressed in the books I knew about or then proceeded to research.

For example, several women told me that the actual experience of being a mother, whatever its concomitant woe, was better than anything they'd ever dreamed of. But, I wondered, did all girls dream of having children? Do some mothers regret the experience? Anyhow, what's the relationship between what women expect from marriage and what they get? How do early daydreams, role models, and the images in the larger culture affect marriages? How do expectations influence the way women choose their husbands? Are the men they marry like the men they dreamed of ? As girls, did they see themselves married and in careers? Married and rich? Is there a connection between romantic dreams and later happiness?

These and similar questions eventually developed into the more formal study on which this book is based. The book is about the women I spoke with. It reports and examines what they said without attempting to draw broad generalizations or to find "objective" truth. For example, there's surely another side to this woman's judgment of her ex-husband: "He makes Hitler look like someone you'd like to have dinner with. He makes Saddam Hussein look gentle." The question of objectivity also arises in the words of a well-known judge: "I could never have done this if my husband had wanted me to be like the other wives we knew." These remarks, for the very reason that they are so personal, are what we need to understand the women's view of their own lives. And beyond that, the common elements in their stories give us a patch of ground to use as a starting place for exploring the larger scene.

I spent about a year traveling through the United States, to cities, towns, and suburbs, meeting with about a hundred women and concentrating intensely on about half that number. Virtually everyone I saw talked thoughtfully and apparently freely, knowing that their names would not be used and that their identities would be disguised. I also think they spoke openly because I rarely laid eyes on their husbands, saying barely more than "hi" if I did catch a glimpse of them. There's another factor: Though women think about their marriages a great deal, they talk about them to family and friends much less than they talked about relationships when they were single; it can feel like a betrayal to discuss your acknowledged partner with people who know you both. I was welcomed as a sounding board, a sympathetic stranger who would come in, listen—and then go away.

The actual interviews were guided by the forty pages of questions I eventually developed. They commonly took any-where from three to nine hours, sometimes spread over a few days. Still, even these more structured encounters retained the quality of the woman-to-woman personal talk of the original conversations: The respondents and I were exchanging confi-dences. When it was relevant, when I thought it would encourage rather than inhibit the flow of their thoughts, I told them about my own life or the lives of my friends.

The subject of marriage expectations and realities seemed to intrigue people. "I haven't thought of that for years!" was a refrain during the talks. I heard things like: "It was my chance to get a lot of stuff off my chest"; or "I thought it over very carefully before I agreed to talk to you"; or "Once I said I'd do it, I made up my mind that I wasn't going to hold back. I was going to answer your questions and get what I could out of it." The opposite reaction also occurred: Apparently verbalizing for the first time something negative about her marriage, a woman would ask: "Has anyone else said this?" And I once heard myself say to a bitterly weeping New Englander whose marriage had been a torture: "Look, it's only a book. We don't have to talk about any of this."

Most often we met in the women's homes, in city apartments, cottages, suburban split-levels, and historic homes. Some of these places were so neat that my papers and equipment seemed like a sloppy intrusion. On the other hand, one young bride, whose living room was strewn with socks and books and apple cores, grinned when she ushered me in and solemnly recited, "A neat house is the sign of a wasted life."

By the time I finished the interviews, I had hours of tapes and miles of transcripts. Nevertheless, themes began to emerge, themes the women themselves had emphasized. For, despite the variety of subjects we explored, each person talked longest about what she believed was most relevant to her own marriage. That's what she kept coming back to.

Among the first things I learned was that except for girls with severely disturbed, usually alcoholic fathers, everyone assumed that growing up meant getting married. That assumption came from the world around them, from family pressure, and from adults, some of whom were role models, some anti-models: "This person is what I most emphatically do not want to grow up to be."

But there were two different kinds of girlhood expectations: The first grows out of the daydreams of the "sleepwalkers," women who drift into marriage under the spell of unexamined girlhood romance. Another group of women, the "calculators"— even though they may be quite young—make specific connections between marriage choices and the life they want for themselves. They pick their husbands under these ground rules and then rely not on daydreams of the future but on plans for getting the kind of marriage they want. As one woman said, "When I first met him, I probably thought that we would live happily ever after, but that's not what guided me. It was more— okay, how to live happily ever after is to make the following plans and act on them."

When you compare the happiness of marriages of women who didn't do much girlhood daydreaming with those who did, the two factors seem cemented together: Dream a lot, your chances for a happy marriage go down; add to that parents whose marriage you consider bad and the prognosis gets worse. You have to be very lucky, as a few women were, to avoid the pitfalls of that combination.

Most of the women were in love when they married. They believe that without that "stored electricity" you can't be happy. And they are apparently right. Not one woman who married without being in love had a happy marriage. The tricky part, as we'll see, is to figure out the conditions that nurtured "falling" in love.

A majority of the people I interviewed married men from their own religious and racial group. Though women who married "outside" tend to blame that factor for later problems, I found that unhappily married respondents who stayed *within* their group blame bad temper, incompatibility, infidelity, and/or abuse. Women in bad "mixed" marriages, after they mention the otherness factor, give the same reasons.

- Certain of the themes that emerged startled me. For example, only a relatively small percentage of the women feel

they have an active and satisfying sex life. How much that matters to them is related to generation: The youngest women care
the least. When we talked about sexual expectations, I heard
repeatedly about a concept I came to call the "playing field of
sex"—the sense the women had of their own bodies as the geography on which the sexual act takes place. It's an idea that helps
to illuminate what we all at some point have observed about
body image, about initiating sex, about the possibility of a
gender imbalance in sexual desire—the common belief that
"men want it more."

Though daydreaming about marriage gets in the way of good
decisions, among the women I saw, daydreaming about work
seemed to lay the groundwork for a productive career. Dream
about career, see yourself outside the home doing important
work—and that's most likely to happen. In the end, however,
when they talked about what they wanted out of work, high-
fliers as well as women in modest jobs came around to asking,
"But will it make me happy?"

Most of the women said that money was important in neither their girlhood expectations nor their evaluation of candidates for a husband. However, as girls, they saw themselves in
lives that included big houses or apartments, minivans, dining
rooms, time for culture, and creative motherhood. They were
foreseeing a style of life that costs the considerable amount of
money they kept themselves from thinking about.

And women commonly mentioned the connection between
their husband's self-respect and his earning power. They say
they don't care about money but they do care about a man
having "his financial act together." Those women who entered
marriage understanding that they might be major breadwinners
concede that they ask of their husbands certain accommodations they would not ask of "a major moneymaker." Work around
the house, child care . . . much of this daily duty seems to be
considered inappropriate for the rich and powerful. On the
other hand, some women, whether or not they have children,

have walked away from high-income jobs much more freely than they believe their husbands would have done. That pattern grows directly out of girlhood expectations about who supports the family.

As to motherhood, it was as if women in a mining town in Montana, a glitzy Los Angeles canyon, a Chicago penthouse over the lake, or a religious South Carolina community were on a modem hookup, so similar was the way they described the joy the experience gave them. A woman with two kids under three said, "Having a baby is the one area of my life where the fantasy was not as good as the reality." But along with the joy came the traditional expectation that it was the mother who would have basic control of child rearing. That turns out, for many people, to be part of an unspoken bargain about who will do most of the work of child care and, on the other side, who will run the financial show.

Common wisdom has it that arranged marriages became extinct in this country in the nineteenth century. In fact, though few couples spell out the details in advance, they proceed as if a marriage contract is in place, as if they know exactly the deal they're making when they walk down the aisle. However, since the contract terms are usually unspoken, it is only after the wedding that people discover that the partners had in mind different clauses governing married life—stipulations that don't necessarily fit together. In any case, as the years pass, the original terms may no longer serve. Unless a system for accommodating change or stretching the contract is in place, trouble ensues. And though it's too early to predict the outcome, there's a real difference in the way young women approach prenuptial negotiation and the way their mothers did. Many of the young women, in effect, negotiate their own marriages.

We'll consider in the separate chapters the details of expectations and realities in the choice of mate, sexuality, children, work, money, and the marriage contract. In the last chapter we'll take a quick look at the girlhood expectations of individual women and balance them against what they themselves consider to be the theme of their marriages. Though perhaps they are dramatized a bit, as codas often are, these themes are like a great deal of what I was being told: thoughtful, interesting, and remarkably free of pretense.

In the hours we visited together, the women I interviewed cast a bright light on what dreams of marriage are made of— and what they come to.

A BRIEF DESCRIPTION OF THE RESPONDENTS

I found the women who appear in this book through a procedure that involved contacting a disparate group of people from various professions, religions, ethnic and age groups . . . whom I knew or learned about in each geographic area. I told them about the project and asked them to provide names of possible interviewees. Then I preinterviewed by telephone and selected those who fit the criteria of the study. Sometimes local groups or the interviewees themselves put me on to people in their localities, who put me on to other people.

Who are these women? They come from every region of the country, from California, Massachusetts, Montana, New York, Texas, Illinois, New Mexico, South Carolina . . . and points north, south, east, and west. At the time I interviewed them, they ranged in age from twenty-six to sixty-nine. Their marriages* took place between 1946 and 1991. They come from a variety of ethnic and religious backgrounds: There are white, black, and Asian women of Protestant, Catholic, and Jewish background. (Religion, ethnicity, and sexual orientation aren't noted in the text unless they're relevant to the subject at hand.)

---

* Unless otherwise indicated, "marriage" means first marriage. And though the term is sometimes used to describe other kinds of relationships, I am referring to legal, heterosexual marriages.

All the women are now or have been married. Over half of them have stayed married to their first husbands. Of those who divorced, more than half have remarried. A few older women are widows. Some divorced women are now in relationships but unmarried; some have turned to a lesbian life; some remain unattached. These bare facts are very close to those that describe the larger American middle-class population.

The specifics of the women's lives with respect to children, work, and money appear in the appropriate chapters. In general most of them have children, most work outside the home, and all have spent some time in college. The large majority have bachelor's degrees, and several have professional degrees or specialized training. All the respondents are middle class: They come from families that, at the time of their marriages, were in the country's median economic and social range. (After talking with several very rich and very poor women, I realized that their lives raise so many special issues that it would be confusing to consider them in this book.)

The identities of the people I interviewed have been disguised, their names changed. The places they live, though not the sections of the country, have sometimes been scrambled to protect their anonymity. Their "stats" are largely unchanged: These include the age at the time I saw them, years married, number of children, education, race, and religion.

2

GROWING UP MEANS GETTING MARRIED

We think of ourselves as living in a time when life-style options are wide open. We see or hear about people who have chosen household arrangements their grandparents didn't have available to them, had not even imagined. But traditional family life is still ubiquitous. Real estate ads feature a cute child on the shoulders of a rugged father whose free arm encircles a beautiful wife. Thanksgiving celebrations in TV commercials don't show a table of single adults holding hands, saying grace. Society, family, friends, the media . . . all the forces that have traditionally shaped the expectations of young people, push them to marry, make them feel that to miss out on marriage is to miss out on the best life has to offer.

> The system works. Almost every respondent assumed she would marry. Despite reservations she may have had along the way, her basic expectation was that growing up meant getting married.

Of course I only interviewed women who had at some point married and who did so before they were forty. It may be that other women operate from a different premise. And middle-class children primarily see around them married adults, so it makes sense that, when they're small, they expect their lives to take that form. But into adulthood, and with remarkable consistency, the women I spoke to saw marriage in their future.

That was true even of Norma who, since her divorce, has lived in a lesbian relationship and who suspects that she was always more interested in women than in men. At fifty-one Wendy has grown children as well as grandchildren. An excellent athlete, well coordinated, quick in her movements, she dresses in bright-colored, handwoven fabrics. Wendy's direct gaze and emphatic manner of speaking make her a strong presence: "I never dreamed for a minute that I wouldn't get married. That was not an option I thought about, being alone. I can't think of a single woman from my childhood who wasn't married. I didn't play girl games and I didn't have a lot of dolls, but I always knew I wanted children. Marriage just came along in the bargain—you can't have a family without having a husband. And the way it worked out, all three of my close college friends married when we were nineteen or twenty. Even at that age we thought that the people who didn't get married were failures in some way and that we were the successful ones. We'd gotten to the right place. From the time I was a small child, being married was what you were meant to do. Everything else was extra."

Christine, forty, is a television executive in her third marriage. She is slim, with well-cut long black hair and bright brown skin. When I saw her in her Hollywood office, she was wearing jeans, a print tank top, and the confident demeanor of somebody who's always been great looking: "There are some women who feel like they can't function unless they have a man. I've never been that kind of person, but when I think about it honestly, I always had a man, I always had the pick. So maybe that's why, even though marriage wasn't consciously my goal, it seemed like it was inevitable. I mean you just took it for granted: You were a good little girl, grew up, went to school, married Mr. Right, had Right kids, and lived happily ever after."

Linda, a talented painter of thirty-seven, has a negative self-image she often refers to. Nevertheless, like Christine, she always assumed she'd marry: "My dad, unfortunately, used to tell me I'd never get married. He thought I was unattractive. Really he told me I was fat and ugly. But had I not gotten married it would have been awful for me. I would have had to really adjust to that, figure it out. It never occurred to me that I could be happy without being married."

The Problem Father

Are there any women who did not assume they'd marry? Helen is one of them. A New York public relations executive, she married for the first time at thirty-six: "For a long time I was sure I did not want to marry, absolutely not—because my father was an alcoholic. He didn't actually abuse us children physically, but the threat of violence that was in the air was terrifying. I am very close with my mother and always very protective of her and I used to pray that he would die. If there was any obsession in my life, it was the issue of being trapped and dependent—even if the alcohol wasn't the problem. I never wanted to find myself without options, where I couldn't handle things myself. That was the reason I didn't even think about getting married until pretty recently."

> **Almost every woman who did not assume that she would marry was the child of a severely disturbed father, most commonly an alcoholic.**

Daughters of such fathers were afraid for their mothers and for themselves. They said they were determined to avoid their mother's "terrible mistake." Women with difficult mothers, on the other hand, seemed to think they were so different from their moms that they didn't have to rule marriage out. In fact, some women with abusive fathers found it easier to explain or forgive their father's behavior than their mother's.

Hilda is sixty-five, but when she talks about her childhood, her voice still carries a tone of both self-mockery and pain: "I loved my mother and I admired her. I felt she was vastly superior to my father. He was weak, he was argumentative. When I went to therapy years later, the shrink kept trying to get me to say that I was angry at my father for sexually molesting me after my mother died, but I wasn't. It was very unpleasant but, you know, I was always sorry for him. I was angry at my mother, that she died, that she left me as a young kid to have to fend with this, because my father couldn't help himself."

THE PRESSURE TO MARRY
Parents

Why is the impetus to marry so strong that virtually everyone takes for granted that growing up means getting married? First is the powerful part the family plays. Though they seldom said it in so many words, parents did convey an insistent promarriage message, as this forty-year-old describes: "I was a career woman until I got married, and my mother was kind of proud of me. I had the apartment in the city, the good job. She would come and stay with me every once in a while, and I think she got a kick out of it. But I always really knew what was in the back of her mind. When my husband and I eloped, I called my mother and she said she was relieved. She'd been worried because ultimately, you're a failure if you don't get married."

And from an engineer of West Indian background: "My mother never did anything quite like talking about my sisters and me getting married but, of course, we had to learn how to cook—and the idea underneath was because we had to cook for our husbands. We had to learn how to clean properly because a man's not going to want you if you can't keep a nice house. So there was always that going on even though it wasn't in words."

Friends

It was her friends who urged Sandra to marry. With a mentally disturbed father, she was one of the few girls who did not assume she would someday marry. Involved in her career, Sandra was content to live alone, acquire nice things, have an occasional affair: "My friends were getting married and though I didn't care about that, they were all after me. One close friend told me it was terrible to stay single and I thought, well, maybe I should. The man I was dating at the time was so nice, he was the closest thing to someone I could marry."

The Passing Years

Contemporary women marry, on average, later than their mothers did, but, in every generation, unless she married relatively early, there came a moment when a woman said, "I'd better do it soon." As the following excerpts show, the date of the anxiety attack is later now than it used to be, but the feeling that you'd better get going, better get married, remains the same:

"A lot of my friends got married around twenty-one and I was worried about whether it would ever happen to me." (55)

"The early part of my twenties were a lot of fun, but in the late part there was a sort of desperate edge. I woke up one day at twenty-nine and said, 'Hey, you're supposed to get married, you're supposed to have kids.' I got married before that year was over." (42)

"I felt like time was running out, I did feel that. I was twenty-five and had been teaching for four years and there weren't many men around. Nobody talked about it but I think my mother worried that if I didn't marry, I might go in the convent, and she didn't really think that was such a great idea." (69)

"When I met my husband, I was twenty-three and he was twenty-five. I was crazy about him, but I was not in the getting-married mode. The plan I had set for myself was: I was going to be having this apartment, and maybe in four or five years get married, and I was going to have kids when I was thirty-three. But my husband was ready and that scared me. I didn't want to lose him, but yet I felt nervous because it was way ahead of my schedule." (28)

Timing, Career, and Kids

The younger women got out of college expecting to work first and think about husband and children later. They were concentrating on career at just the age their mothers had concentrated on marriage. Though the older women may have expected to work, they commonly said things like,"I don't want to be tied down when I'm older. I'll put child rearing behind me and then get on with my own life." Beginning a family when you were thirty-five was uncommon. If you waited too long, they believed, you would "have less patience, you wouldn't be able to get down on the floor and play with your kids." Your baby might be born with an impairment. There were whispers of "change-of-life babies," "accidents" by women who mistakenly thought they were safe from pregnancy.

When women began to defer child rearing, they also deferred marriage—up to the point that biology set off the alarm on the ticking clock. Then, as their mothers sometimes had found they were late to easily start a career, their daughters sometimes found they were late to easily get pregnant.

> **Whatever the timing, their strong desire for children pushed women of all generations to marry.**

Donna is a thirty-six-year-old Californian from Central America with bright olive skin and dark hair with an auburn aura. She wears expensive clothes with a casual, take-it-or-leave-it chic. Donna has a trim body but, right now, the full breasts of a nursing mother. You can hear on the recording of our conversation the gurgling and cooing of her redheaded baby. Here's how Donna would screen her suitors: "I wanted to get a T-shirt printed BORN TO BREED and use it to scare away people who didn't want children. I really knew that what I wanted was a family, and to be able to give them a good life. I'd meet men that liked me, wanted to be married, but didn't want to have children, and I'd say, 'Well, I'm sorry, that's not what my plans are.'"

Sex

In chapter 5 we'll see the role their own sexual needs played in the older women's decision to marry. For now, a sample from a woman of sixty-two who was a virgin when she married at twenty-five: "I was at the point where I said that I didn't want to step outside and get hit by a truck and not know what sex was all about."

The Way Out

Many women chose to marry in order to escape the circumstances in which they found themselves.

Some people simply had no place to go. We heard Anne describe how she married ahead of her schedule because her husband happened to turn up. But her description of the years just before marriage offer another insight: "My parents separated when I was in eleventh grade, and my mother and sister and I moved out of our house. Then my dad remarried and brought the new family to live there. This house on the beach had been my home, and then it wasn't anymore. I started realizing I had to make my own home. It was the same about money. After the divorce my parents basically said, for college you have to figure out what you're going to do and how you're going to pay for it. Even though I married when I was about a year after school, I was actually married—I mean I was actually taking care of myself—from the time I was seventeen."

Because her father was so abusive, her mother so submissive, Lucy, thirty-six, was living with her grandmother when she met her husband-to-be but: "I was forced to go back to my parents again and there was no way I was going to stay in the same house with them. My boyfriend and I'd had a great year in the city together getting to know each other, but I mean this is the 1970s we're talking about, I'm a strong feminist, and I thought I would *never* get married. I just didn't believe it was necessary. But because of our age difference—he was over twenty-one, I was just barely seventeen—it was a felony, a Mann Act offense or something, for him actually to be with me. My father threatened us, so my husband came down and technically kidnapped me and we got married."

Women from much less extreme situations married to gain independence from their parents, especially in the days before living on your own or "living together" was widely accepted. But consider Zoë, now thirty-six, who moved in with her boyfriend when she was twenty-four: "My boyfriend and I lived together for some months but my mother wasn't ready for the new day. She was putting a lot of pressure on me, getting my uncles to call: 'You're killing your mother, Zoë. It's shameful.'"

Rachel, a forty-five-year-old Mississippian, married at twenty-three to escape an uncertain future: "I was afraid of supporting myself. I knew that if I didn't get married I probably had to teach but not because I liked it, only because I didn't know what else to do. My husband was the one I was in love with at that moment when it was all coming together but the fact that I didn't quite know what to do next played a big role. He was a very eligible man who also made me feel secure. That's the big difference between me and the people—even here in the South—who were younger, who did not need a man to make them feel secure. It wasn't just the financial security I was looking for, it was somebody who was going to take care of me. Period."

Amy, a distinguished scientist of twenty-eight, is the kind of independent young woman Rachel refers to but another fear motivated her: "I was influenced at a very young age by the women's movement, so that even though I assumed I was going to get married, I never had fantasies that someone was going to take care of me, ever. I was always going to take care of myself. I work and I know how to rent an apartment and buy a car and do all the things you need to do. Whether I would be happy is an entirely different story. I really do need and crave companionship. Sometimes when I'm alone I feel almost unreal. It doesn't get to be real until I can talk to someone about it, and most of the time that's my husband."

Natalie, divorced and with grown children, was a Jewish child in Holland during the German occupation: "My parents managed to sustain a way of life that kept me relatively sane. I remember frightful things happening and being aware of them, but I don't remember inordinate fear. There were soldiers, there were people being killed, there were atrocities, and walking past the Gestapo building and hearing screams. I suppose out of that history, at the age of nineteen when I married, it was comforting to follow the classic pattern: You move out of your parents' home into the home of somebody else who will take care of you and make decisions. I wanted the safety. Being married would be a safe place. There may have been a part of me that said, 'Hey, if I can get married and avoid that in-between of being on my own, won't that be terrific?' Because I was really scared."

I'm Pregnant

....

If you're not married and reject abortion or adoption, there's no shove down the aisle so compelling as an unplanned pregnancy.

....

At thirty-four Rita has two sons, nine and twelve. The older boy is extraordinary looking, with pale blond curly hair, bold features, and the carriage of an Olympic runner. Rita said: "I thought I would be older than twenty-one, maybe in the thirties or forties, before I got married. When I got pregnant that rushed the whole thing. My father was a minister in a small town, and when I called him, I began crying: 'I just messed up, I just did something so stupid.' My dad piped in and asked, 'Have you asked God to forgive you for doing what you did?' and when I said I had, he answered, 'Then let's go on with life. Now we've got to deal with you and how you're going to take it.'

"I was living with a bunch of girls who were frequently having sex, and they never got pregnant. It's ironic because then all of a sudden they look at me like I was the bad one. I knew my husband about a year and we only had sex once, one night when we'd had a little too much to drink. It was the first time for both of us and the next day we decided that we didn't have fun and that we really didn't want to pursue it. I know that sounds like, 'Oh, right, sure, everybody says that,' but no, this was really true.

"When it turned out I was pregnant, I immediately called an abortion clinic. But everybody around me, not knowing my problem, was talking about how bad abortion was. And then, at the dentist, my boyfriend saw this magazine with the different stages of the fetus. That night he came over, and we both agreed that we were going to have this baby. We made that choice. My parents were supportive but it was the worst way to start out. Like for the wedding, we picked up the cheapest dress and got a hat, and my mother put a little pink flower on it so it wouldn't be all white. That kind of bothered her, she needed to tarnish it up a little bit."

Carol, forty-two, lives in San Diego with her history-professor husband. A popular caterer, Carol has the look and style of a Frenchwoman, with neat features, a cap of reddish brown hair, and a very personal fashion sense. She lives in a rambling house whose center is a large Spanish-style kitchen. Like Rita's, Carol's voice is tinged with bitterness when she talks about the circumstances of her marriage: "I married when I was twenty-nine, twenty-nine and pregnant. The combination was a powerful impetus. My fantasy had been that we would go out together for a year or two, and then we would see.

"And then, suddenly, I'm pregnant. The pressure was on—what do we do? I felt that I had three options: I could get an abortion, have the baby as a single mother, or I could marry my husband. The friend I discussed it with said, 'Look, forget about raising this kid by yourself. Are you out of your mind?' The thing was, I didn't really want to have an abortion. I had had two other abortions. I don't know scientifically what's been proven, but my thought was, God, if you keep having abortions, it's going to make it more difficult when you really want to have a baby. And anyhow, this was a baby I wanted, this baby was going to live.

"My boyfriend couldn't believe it when I told him. Here was this woman he's dating for three months, and I tell him I'm pregnant. The way the decision was finally made, after a few weeks he kind of came out and said, 'Do whatever you need to do, but I can't do this.' I was in a total state. I had a big emotional outburst and told him, 'Fine, I'm out of here. Don't try to date me, just forget about it, it's over.' He came back and proposed a day later and we got married. But I think he was rightfully panicked. He was coming from no responsibility, really, a single guy, a college instructor, to having a wife and child. Neither of us was prepared for that. We didn't know what we were getting ourselves into. It's a terrible way to get married. It took us the first ten years of our marriage to get over it."

....

The pressure to marry came from every direction, and without giving it a thought, women took as a given that they eventually would. Except for those with severely dysfunctional fathers, no one allowed herself to consider the value of marriage as an institution or whether it was appropriate for her as an individual. This meant that in their eagerness to take the step, women sometimes picked the wrong person. And, as we'll next consider, they did not examine or articulate the kind of future they themselves wanted. The result was that they had no way of knowing whether the marriage they were making would help them achieve a satisfying life.

3

DREAMS AND EXPECTATIONS

s I traveled around the country, I began to understand that there is a difference between assuming you'll marry and daydreaming about it. Having expectations means that you can make plans to fulfill them. Daydreams, on the other hand, emit a pink fog that obscures your goal and makes it hard to reach.

Perhaps because I myself was the Compleat Daydreamer until I was forty-five, it took me a while to recognize the connection between girlhood dreams and marriage. Certainly I'd seen few references to it except in novels. But, as it developed, there were clear lines to be drawn between the lives of women who dreamed their way into marriage and those who made plans.

The accounts of two women take us directly into the girlhood background of marriage. Rachel and Barbara are of the same generation and come from an apparently similar southern background. Their families, however, functioned very differently, as do their own marriages. In the highlighted passages that follow we'll see that, between them, these women touch on most of the dreams and expectations that have later influence on marriage.

RACHEL

First, let's walk through the tree-lined historic district of a small Mississippi town to Rachel's meandering eighteenth-century house. Rachel is forty-five, and, even at home, despite the ninety-five-degree southern spring heat, she wears stockings and pumps. A graceful conversationalist, she speaks with a strong local accent but without the colorful metaphors so common in this part of the country: *"The thought that I would not get married never occurred to me.* It would have seemed very lonely to me. So many things in my childhood revolved around things done as a family and as a couple. *I always daydreamed about marriage, and from the time I was a little girl we played dressing up and getting married.* We sometimes talked about having children but we didn't ever think about what it meant, the sex. *As to the husband, he just wasn't in the picture, there was just a nebulous somebody in the background.*

"I greatly admired a friend of my parents' who taught me in Sunday School one year. She was beautiful and she had five beautiful children and a beautiful home. In a way I wanted to grow up to be like her, but there was another woman who'd been Phi Beta Kappa at Duke. She was an intellectual, as the first woman was not. *A cross between those two was what I wanted to be, but definitely married.*

"Because my parents worked together professionally, they talked about their work, about what they were doing in the yard, they did flower arranging together, they went to dances together. Daddy also would make my brother and me get up and wash the dishes, and on Sunday mornings, when the maid wasn't there, he'd say, 'We're going to make the beds now.' He never thought that it was my mother who was going to do it.

"Which I don't have. *I think I assumed, coming out of that climate, that my marriage would run like my parents', where my husband would be boss like my father was, but the decisions and the work would be shared.* In our marriage the assumption was that my husband was earning the real money and I was going to stay home and keep the house. And about the dancing? We've talked a lot about how we go to something and he doesn't ask me to dance. It makes me feel like the skinny little wallflower I was when I was in the seventh grade.

"My husband used to say that if my father told me to jump, I would say, 'How high?' I did fear my father, his sternness. *But the truth is that though I've gotten so I do it less than I used to, I also do still defer to my husband more than he does to me. It's a carryover from how I was with my father.* And it was the same in Mother's family. My mother had wanted to be a doctor or a nurse but her father would not allow it. When the price dropped out of cotton, her father lost everything, and Mother had to drop out of school so her younger brother could finish college. *While women in Mother's family were highly valued, they were expected to defer to the man and there were limited expectations for them.* They weren't given a middle name on the assumption that they were going to get married and their middle name was going to be their maiden name.

"*When I was a teenager I really did think that I was going to live like a Doris Day or Grace Kelly movie. I did not conscientiously sit down and think: These are the things I want to do in life.* I want a partnership kind of marriage, so I'd better be looking for someone who wants to travel and likes to go out and likes to read books and talk about them. I never did that."

BARBARA

Barbara, also in her mid-forties, lives in a similar tiny, historic town, but in Georgia. A chemist, Barbara has an English complexion, curly hair that is a bright premature white, and a self-confident bearing that makes her seem taller than she is. She expresses her strong views emphatically but with humor. She and her husband have an old house that has been lovingly restored and expanded. The furnishings, particularly in the original parlor, are good family pieces.

Barbara says: "*I didn't do that much daydreaming, maybe just a Cinderella-type thing once in a while, but there was never a question in my mind that I would marry.*

"Although she was a stay-at-home mom, my mother had her limits, her standards. *My parents had what I considered a harmo-*

nious marriage but every now and then, if my dad went one step too far, she'd say, 'This is far enough. I'm doing this, this, and this; you can do this, this, and this.' She was loving, nurturing, all those things, but she was never willing to be a doormat. And my daddy really respected her.

"My mother wasn't a diamond-earring type, always telling me to brush my hair and get my umbrella. She just wasn't a naggy kind of a mama but, when she gave you advice, it was worth listening to. *First of all she advised me to marry someone at least as smart as I am or at least as well educated. The second was to marry somebody who puts me first.* She did that and so did I. There's no doubt about it. I come before my husband's job, before his children, before his mother. I am number one in his life.

"By the time I got married I had a pretty good idea of what I did and did not want. My father was a snorer, and I always said, 'I will never marry anybody that snores.' And so I got a little line: 'I'll never marry anybody that does this, I'll never marry anybody does that.' My mother said, *'Listen, you'd better marry somebody quickly because you're getting pickier by the year. Eventually there'll be nobody perfect enough for you.'* But it was from her I learned to figure what I wanted out of life and then go get it."

THE WOMEN IN YOUR LIFE

The mothers of Rachel and Barbara had a lot to do with their expectations of marriage; Rachel also mentioned two other women whom she admired and wanted to grow up to be like.

The adults in their lives helped shape the women's image of marriage. They were, however, influenced by people they admired as well as by the anti-models, those they decidedly did not want to emulate.

Rita, a thirty-four-year-old midwestern kindergarten teacher, talked a lot about her aunt: "She was a single parent and yet she carried on like it was okay, and I thought that was really neat. My aunt taught and went to school herself and then got this big job in the private sector. Later on she always had the latest fads in her house and she just seemed kind of cool and with-it. Lots of things she does, you have to say how wonderful they are. On the other side, my aunt was always very focused on herself and her own accomplishments, not on her children. I don't want to be like that. I want to focus on the family and enjoy life. I don't want to give that away like I saw her do when I was a kid."

Teachers and athletic coaches were often role models. Donna, from Central America, said: "My teacher's name was Milagra and she was my perfect image, she was my idol, because it wasn't my mom I wanted to copy. She's a business-woman and she loved money more than she loved being married and having a family. Milagra was tall and lean and graceful. Her house was really clean and her children were cute, and I wanted to be just like her when I grew up and got married."

Older relatives or family friends also had a strong influence, with mothers functioning both as role models and anti-models. Doris, sixty-nine, wears her white hair in what used to be called a Buster Brown cut. Her petite size and chirpiness make it hard to remember that she is an authority in the social service field. She lives in Seattle in an old house that is full of wonderful stuff—a bottle collection, lots of plants, two exquisitely stitched embroideries her mother did, one a flower-covered tribute to the city, another that reads SOCIALISM IS THE FUTURE OF THE WORLD: "My mother was a businesswoman, but also she nurtured the family. I looked up to her, truly. She and her friends were very strong and I was sort of in awe of some of the idealistic and unconventional things they did. My mother is the person in my life that I model after. It's true to this day though she's long gone."

Christine, the television producer, said: "I guess my mother was as good a wife as she could be to a gambler and a womanizer. If anything, maybe she was too good, because she bailed him out so many times. I'd never put up with the stuff she did. I was always careful to stay away from a situation like that."

Martha's mother was considered not quite the wife her professional husband merited, and there are resonances of that model in Martha's own marriage. Martha lives near the law school at which her husband teaches, in an elegant old building. Her apartment is huge, filled with antiques that are largely a legacy of her parents' travels. She wears no makeup and her matte black hair is plainly styled. Her clothes are also dark, her demeanor unusually settled for someone of fifty-one, her voice so soft that to get my otherwise serviceable tape recorder to pick up what she was saying, we had to put it in her lap: "In my family there was an enormous anxiety about getting a match for one's daughter, in that my mother's success would be bound up in my getting married successfully. In fact I became the good daughter because I married a lawyer, I made the right decision, and I made them happy with me. I didn't have to do almost anything else because I did that.

"It was our parents who fixed us up. My husband's father and mine were in the same profession and they thought we'd make a good match. From the time I met him I wanted to marry him, but he was indifferent at that stage of his life and unready for commitment or commitment to me, whatever. I think that set the pattern for my being more needy emotionally in our marriage. I kept feeling like I needed to prove myself all the time, that I was good enough for him—as I had with my parents. I never wanted to end up like my mother who was sort of a trapped artist in a way, and also trapped in a marriage where she had little equality."

Martha seems resigned to the power structure of her marriage though she has been coming into her own professionally, having recently finished a long and arduous course of study. Her husband's reaction to her hard-won degree? "Maybe this will make you a more interesting person."

DAYDREAMS AND LET'S-PRETEND GAMES

As we'll see in later chapters, it was not only marriage the women dreamed of. They also had fantasies of children, sex, Olympic triumphs, and a house with beautiful paintings and a view of the sea. Women imagined being rich and famous and having a brilliant career—all the while married.

> About half the women had frequent daydreams about marriage. These tended to focus on the setting, the style of life, the children. As we'll explore in chapter 4, neither pretend games nor fantasies had much to do with a husband. If a man was present, he was rarely a well-rendered person.

A few excerpts of the daydreams follow. As you'll see from the women's ages (in parentheses, after each quote), the dreams are remarkably similar from generation to generation:

"I kind of had the image of the knight in shining light, the white knight in the shining armor who would rescue me from the hard times I had with my parents. But I never had a real picture of him. Really, I never got beyond the wedding." (34)

"My ideal was the children and the dog and the station wagon." (62)

"I thought I was going to be spending the rest of my life with plants, and kids running around, and dogs in the minivan. It was this great big friendly, bucolic, idyllic scene." (43)

"I was really focused on the marriage image. Every weekend when we visited, my grandmother and I would get cut-out dolls and play wedding. I would draw pictures of my kids, all nine of them, with their names and their hobbies. Tommy and Katy were the youngest." (27)

"My image of marriage was standing outside and looking into somebody's dining room. The mother is setting the table and the father is talking to her. They're getting ready for a family dinner, and there's a kid somewhere, and I see them all playing games together after dinner." (58)

In addition to such fantasies, girls used "let's-pretend" games to dream out loud. They would playact with friends or relatives, sometimes with dolls, sometimes with only their imagination supplying the props. Joyce, a Texan actress of fifty-three, talks affectionately about her own "hippie days." There is something in her appearance of those days—an embroidered shirt, jeans, and long wavy blond hair in what is probably the style she's always worn. The childhood games Joyce describes had their echoes everywhere I traveled, among women of all groups: "We played with our dolls who usually had scarlet fever and got kidnapped and murdered. The husbands were not present but I did have one cousin about my age and when he came to visit we used to play, all very innocently, that we were married. He was a coal miner or a fireman and he'd go off to work and do his things, and when our parents would tell us it was time to go home, we would have a closing scene where a messenger would come in and tell me my husband had been killed in an explosion. That'd be the end of it. We'd finish and go home."

Where Dreams Come From

The women I spoke to have a wise and rueful understanding that their fantasies derive from the culture around them. They could pinpoint the threads from which they'd spun their images of married life. For example, contrasting her present life to her daydreams, Linda says: "My husband and I blend pretty well together but marriage isn't what I thought it would be. Marriage is struggle, the two words are synonymous. But! We're not told that. I grew up with the lies that marriage is a sweet wonderful thing. Not going by my family—what I saw at home wasn't sweet and wonderful—but I was really brought up by TV and the movies, by advertisements, and the whole culture saying that you melted into each other's arms and had this love relationship that was ever blossoming and growing but somehow never changed. Probably the strongest influence on me was the Beatles' music, 'Michelle, ma belle.' He always loved you and thought you were great, you always loved him and thought he was great. It's not that way at all."

Books helped shape many dreams, though they were seldom mentioned by women now in their twenties. Hilda, sixty-five, says: "I'd be rich, I'd be famous, I'd be beautiful, I'd be talented. I thought I would have it all and I got that idea from books. I read all the time. Books saved my life in one sense—they were an escape from my mother's death, my father's abuse—but they corrupted me terribly. The idea that the man always rescued the woman came from books, and the idea that I was going to be rich. The books were always so glamorous and wonderful, they gave you an escape, you retreated into them."

Women of all ages said that films and/or television were the important influence on their early expectations of marriage. It was here that they got many of their ideas about personal relationships and gender roles. But the media also presented a vivid image of the perks you can look forward to when you marry: Hepburn's town house on the East River; Doris Day's dog, station wagon, and big yard; Diahann Carroll's neat house in a seamlessly integrated neighborhood; the rustic but fully appointed ranch house. "Ozzie and Harriet" was the earliest TV couple mentioned when women were describing or making fun of their early picture of marriage. They also found the raw material of their fantasies in programs like *Little House on the Prairie, Father Knows Best, Leave It to Beaver, Julia, Eight Is Enough, The Partridge Family,* and *The Brady Bunch.*

Christine, the savvy African-American producer, says of the television series of her girlhood: "When I was a kid I wanted the marriages I saw on TV like *Father Knows Best* or *The Donna Reed Show.* I guess I was naive and sheltered; the all-girls Catholic school I went to was very racially mixed. I didn't even realize there was a black movement going on until I went to college. Marcus Garvey could have been a candy bar for all I knew. When I was a kid, I'd look at the screen and I wouldn't think, There's only white people on there. At that time TV was all white, so you just took it for granted."

Let's turn off the TV set with the words of a Japanese-American professor in her early forties who grew up with traditional values so ingrained that they apparently exempted her from the American dream–media connection: "Did I see any marriages I admired? As a young girl? A teenager? Not really, no. On television? Gosh, what was on television? I always would laugh! I didn't say, 'Oh, I want to have a family like that.' Never. I don't ever remember saying that. Why would I?"

THE CONSEQUENCES OF DAYDREAMING

> The large majority of women who frequently fanta-sized about marriage say they had unhappy first mar-riages. More than half the women who seldom daydreamed report happy first marriages.

The Dreamers

Why do frequent romantic girlhood dreams so often predict an unhappy first marriage? Sue Ellen, forty-three, feels that the illusions of her generation led her astray: "I was part of the hip-pies, bohemian I guess was more the word. Because of the ide-alization of the 'Nam era, everything was ideal, things were all just magically supposed to happen. I assumed I'd be madly in love with my husband and we'd gallop off into the sunset and live happily ever after. I had so many dreams and so many ideals. Unfortunately most of them centered around me in rela-tionship to someone else, this very vague person of the male gender who was somehow magically going to make everything just fine. It's been very painful to let go of those illusions in this grim life I lead with my husband."

A Boston foundation administrator of sixty-six explains: "I was a person who daydreamed constantly from the time I was a tiny child. I think I understood in theory that here was a fantasy and here was real life. But when it was time to get married, along came this guy who was handsome and a great athlete—just like my dopey dreams. So I married him. I never thought about it in terms of what life was all about. I didn't say, 'Is he going to make a good husband? Are we going to have a good life together? Do we have the same ideals? Will he be able to earn a living? Be proud of himself?' None of that. Absolutely none."

The Nondreamers

A few women did not fantasize about marriage because their home situation made married life unimaginable, as Carol, the San Diego caterer, explains: "My father was an alcoholic and my mother complained bitterly to me. I was the receptacle and the sounding board for this miserable mistake, so of course I didn't have a lot of fantasies about marriage. In fact, I really forced myself to go the opposite route so I wouldn't get stuck like my mother did. Even during the first years of my own marriage, I expected so little. I think that when you can express what you want from marriage, you do better. Unfortunately for me, I couldn't express it because I'd never seen it."

But there was a much more common pattern among the women who did not daydream: "I always assumed I'd get married but I didn't think about the whole thing too much. I wasn't a dreamy kid; I did things. And I had my parents' example: They might be upset with each other occasionally but never quarreling. Maybe my father would stay out golfing longer on Sunday. He'd say he'd be home at four and it would be six. Those are the only things I can think of they ever fussed about. It was a good marriage, the kind I looked for."

This explanation comes from a woman in Montana but it is very like what I heard from Barbara in Georgia and many other people. These women did not do much fantasizing because the primary marriage they saw, their parents', was fine. They took for granted that a man and a woman could live a good life together, so they didn't give a lot of dream time to the subject: People get married; they're okay.

Popular wisdom has it that modern women are "more realistic" about marriage than women were in the past; that people who marry very young don't know what they're getting into; that city folk have a harder time settling down than do their rural cousins. I found that where fantasies are concerned, there were dreamers as well as nondreamers in all the ethnic, geographic, and generational groups. Nor does the age at which the women married seem to make a difference. There is, however, a recurring crucial connection.

Of the women who—whatever the "objective" reality—considered their parents happy, almost twice as many did not frequently daydream about marriage as did. That was the winning combination: Don't daydream much, rate your parents' marriage happy, and you're likely to have a happy first marriage yourself.

The one exception to this rule seems to clarify and reinforce it: Jeannette's parents were happy, she didn't daydream, but she married and then quickly divorced her first husband. The daughter of a well-known public official, Jeannette deliberately sought a more exciting life than what she saw in the African-American upper middle class: "I didn't dream much about marriage because everyone around me when I was growing up had a good marriage. Nobody ever divorced; my parents were great together. Wherever I went in my little world, someone knew them. As soon as I would mention my family's name, doors would open. I used to say, 'I need to go someplace where no one knows my parents and see what it's like.' I think that's why I went out of the mold for my first husband, picking someone who led a really different kind of life. Now, with my second, I'm back on track and really happy."

The Odds

Does this mean that if you believe your parents' marriage was unhappy you're doomed to a bad marriage yourself? It's important to remember that we are talking here only about *first* marriages. Many of the women with unhappy parents and bad marriages themselves either remarried or are living satisfying unmarried lives. They have taken helpful lessons away from their failed marriages. They also have stopped daydreaming about marriage and have instead focused on the realities they have experienced. If they remarried, they usually picked more carefully and were more attentive to the tricky parts of married life.

But even in first marriages, the unhappy-parents-unhappy-marriage sequence is not inexorable. Something else is going on: Whatever their opinion of their parents' marriage, women who gave practical consideration to what had gone wrong in their birth homes and then deliberately set about avoiding such problems, also avoided disaster in their own marriages.

The women who did best, "the calculators," could articulate what they wanted from marriage and the kind of husband that required. The "sleepwalkers," those who daydreamed a lot, tended to drift unthinkingly into marriage; they had to be extremely lucky to avoid disaster.

4

CHOOSING
A HUSBAND

f all the complex decisions we make in life, selecting a spouse is the most fraught with possibilities for long-term happiness or misery. No matter what our sophistication, we marry believing it's for keeps. Perhaps couples without children, married for only a year or two, have less difficulty dissolving a union than other people do; but there is little chance that even they, walking down the aisle, had their fingers crossed or were taking the commitment casually. Certainly all the women I talked to, whatever later happened, believed their wedding to be celebrating a life-long contract.

I CHOOSE YOU

Most of the women always assumed they'd marry but what made them pick a particular person for so important a role in their lives? And for what reasons do they think their husbands chose them? Because of the unanimity of opinion, let's begin with the second answer:

> **Virtually every woman I spoke to identifies her own energy, cheerfulness, liveliness . . . as the qualities her husband admired.**

People of all generations, ethnicity, and geography use virtually the same vocabulary to express this belief:

"My husband married me because he really was attracted to a certain open spirit I have, a directness and emotionality. He likes the fact that I'm verbal, he really enjoys listening to me."

"He thought I was fun. I was energetic, happy, wanted to laugh a lot, exciting, kind of a risk taker. It wasn't that he didn't want to do those kinds of things, he just needed some prodding."

"My outgoingness, I think, was what attracted him. We met at a sorority dance, and according to him, he picked me out. He wanted to know who was that girl over there talking to everybody. So maybe opposites do attract; in that sense we are very opposite."

"My husband wanted me because I was a menagerie. I was shiny, I was happy, I have a zest for life."

Are these women all charming and witty and gay? Some seem to be, others don't particularly. Though we don't know their husbands, in general, men may be more reserved than women. And perhaps women themselves *expect* and *are expected* by society to bring these qualities to the relationship. It's striking how pleased their voices are, how happy the respondents that they are fun and energetic and outgoing. And the very few women who feel like dull wrens beside glittering males sadly regret it. They worry that they are "dampening their husbands' spirits," not playing their proper role.

The Dream Man

We know from the previous chapter that girls usually skipped a step when they fantasized about marriage.

....

The women could see their kids and their front yards in great detail but the men they'd marry were nebulous figures.

....

The few women who do recall early dream men now laugh about them: "My older sister and I used to pretend that we had a magic closet we could look inside and see the faces of our future husbands. My picture of a husband was a tall, dark man and she always wanted a short man. She'd sort of look in the closet and then turn around and say, 'You'd better not look at who's in here for you.'"

Linda, the thirty-seven-year-old New Jersey painter, said: "When I was a kid I wanted to marry a Beatle. I would always fantasize about one of them coming to our house and finding out that he was madly in love with me, this great person."

Rock Hudson and Cary Grant are mentioned by women in the appropriate generations. A mythic Prince Charming turns up among women of all ages, including this hip young film producer: "I never thought to myself when I was a girl, I want a man with whom I can talk or anything practical like that. I was much more affected by the image of the Prince Charming."

And from the Texan actress of fifty-three: "I used to think that my suitors would be lined up in the living room and my father would choose one for me. And I expected to get everything I needed from my husband, emotionally, physically, financially. He would be my Prince Charming, my love, and we would do everything together—it sounds awful to me now."

Alice, who has remained in an oppressive marriage for more than thirty years, still laughingly imagines the dream man: "I never fantasize about a stranger coming up to my door because he might be in farmer overalls and a bib cap or Ned Beatty instead of Warren. I'd really like someone who looked like the young Henry Fonda, and had a voice like Shelby Foote's—that southern accent—and a way with women like Warren Beatty. I know it's immature but those dream men are out there bigger than life. They don't have any flaws for us to see, and we don't have to pick up their underwear."

The Qualifications

"I never gave any thought before I married to the qualities I wanted in a husband."

"I didn't ever sit down and say, 'If I want this kind of life, I'd better not marry this person.'"

"I don't think I ever really thought through what the man I married would be like because my life happened to me. It isn't as if I created my demands and then went about meeting them."

....

The women who were the dreamers, the "sleepwalkers," did not formulate the specific qualities they wanted in a husband.

....

Unconsciously they must have had standards. They turned candidates down. None of them married men they believed would make bad fathers. No one married a man she thought would be unemployed. But they did not spell out in any detail what they wanted.

This was true even among women now under forty-five, who, you might imagine, would be more thoughtful about the attributes of a husband. But daydreamers in every generation wandered into marriage. It was only *after* they chose a man that the younger women sometimes thrashed out with their future husbands certain aspects of their life together.

....

The women who were "calculators," who knew the characteristics they wanted in a husband, are much more likely to have happy marriages.

....

Are they fooling themselves? Crediting themselves with more foresight than they actually had? Have they, for peace of mind, decided that what they got is what they wanted in the first place? It doesn't seem so. Luck surely played a part but these women do seem to have had definite ideas while they were still single, even though some of them were quite young. They were able to specify in detail or in a short list of essentials the kind of man who would fit into the married life they expected.

One of the qualities such women share (to go back to the previous chapter) is that they did not spend much time dreaming about romance and marriage when they were girls.

Jane, forty-three, has delicate features and is barely five feet tall. The day I spent with her she wore a brilliant red dress of a tie-dyed design. A shellacked wooden sign hangs over the front door of her suburban house with a legend something like, THIS IS AN AMERICAN HOME THAT FOLLOWS SOME JAPANESE-AMERICAN CUSTOMS. PLEASE REMOVE YOUR SHOES BEFORE YOU ENTER, AS WE DO. The thick, pale beige carpets are, needless to say, immaculate.

Jane did not consciously emulate her parents' marriage, but her ideas about family arise from the tradition they embodied: "Even at nineteen, when I met my husband, I felt that we would have a good life together. He is very honest, to-the-penny kind of honest. I remember at a restaurant when we were dating, not being charged for something. Most people would say, "Oh, look, we got this free," but he told the waitress. I was like, ooh, that was something I was looking for. And I knew he would be a good father. Then, I have to seriously say, I did consider what he did because I wanted someone who would make a living. And he is the type who sets a lot of goals. When we were thinking about marriage, he was still a clerk but he told me, 'It's going to take me about four or five years to become office manager. We'll save until we can buy a home.'

"But it wasn't just material things. I could see that ideologically this man had the same ideas I did on what family is about and that it fits into the larger family. To get to this point requires education and all of that, and that's what you have to look for. Because we both knew what we were looking for, we set goals together when we were young. The job, and the house, and that I would work, and we would have children, and be prepared to retire together. We had expectations and we made plans to fulfill them and that's what we worked towards. I think that goes all the way back. The planning is practical rather than romantic. When I first met him, I probably thought that we would live happily ever after, but that's not what guided me. It was more: Okay, how to live happily ever after is to make the following plans and act on them."

From the time she was very young, Barbara, the southern chemist, seems to have rigorously organized her affairs: "After I graduated I'd been working in Oklahoma and I chose a new job because I felt that in a couple of years I would probably meet and marry someone, and if that happened, I didn't want to end up living the rest of my life somewhere like that.

"I wanted someone absolutely 101 percent dependable. My father and my husband? You can set your clock by them as to when they're going to come home. When I first met my husband my guard was sort of up, like the guy's got to pass muster before I'm going to turn loose with my heart. I put a price tag on everything, and I don't mean money. I try to teach my children that everything you do in life has consequences, and you have got to decide whether the reward is worth the risk. And so that's what I kept thinking: Is this somebody I can afford to really get hooked on? At the very beginning, before I let myself go, I wasn't in love where the bells ring and the heart flops and you can't believe this is happening to you. No, it was a rational decision, and then I fell in love. I knew that you can't change people very much. The basic person that you marry is right there."

Barbara stresses that what you see is what you get, probably one of the most important criteria for picking a husband. She and Jane both knew the qualities they were looking for and carefully considered whether the husband candidate had them. Women like these mention looking for intelligence, integrity, a sense of humor. They say they wanted a friend and a good father for their children. Marrying a rich man comes up only once in a while, though they all expected to marry someone who would make a living and would "respect himself" in terms of career and earning power.

The Ethnic Card

Nobody said anything remotely like, "I dreamed of a Prince Charming who was tall and handsome—and Presbyterian"; or "My fantasies were of an athletic blond man who came from this corner of this southern state." Nevertheless:

....

Almost three-quarters of the women married men of the same or a similar background.

....

Maybe they didn't have to include ethnicity in their dreams; maybe, as women assumed that growing up meant getting married, they also assumed it meant marrying someone "of your own kind."

Among the people I talked to, most Catholics married Catholics, Jews married Jews, Protestants of all denominations married Protestants. The pattern also held for most white, black, and Asian women—as it did for respondents from the Deep South, who think of themselves as a separate group, with specifically southern ways that shaped their expectations and relationships.

No parents actually forbade their daughter to marry outside her group, though sometimes they did some manipulation to prevent it or, after the marriage failed, commented that they always had reservations. Perhaps, as one mother said, they were afraid that interfering would alienate the young woman or push her to marry a person they considered inappropriate. But there was parental pressure. One woman, now twenty-nine, says her mother wanted her to marry someone who had the "Three Cs": He should, like her father, be "Cute, Catholic, and have a Career."

Several Protestant women mention their parents' opposition when they seemed to be getting serious about Catholic boys. Joyce, the Texan actress, remembers: "My first year I went to a little liberal arts school but after one year my parents transferred me to State. They said it was because it was a better school but really it was because of some guy I was going with. He was a Catholic. It was amazing to me that they could do that; they just shipped me down there."

Shirley, thirty-four, married her husband *because* of his difference: "I grew up in very much a redneck town and when I was going to school I never saw any other Asians. I was treated badly because I was Chinese. They would call me Jap and other really rude things or sometimes throw things at me. I've always been small, so that made it even worse. I looked different, and then I had this weird last name.

"I was twenty-two when I got married. I didn't tell my parents for several years because my mother had always said that if I didn't marry somebody Chinese, I would be disowned. I don't know how she expected me to meet Chinese boys living where we did. My husband was half black and half white. I was attracted to him because he represented a very different life. There was a certain air about him. It wasn't just physical attraction, but he kind of took me into another world I never even imagined. He had the gift of gab, he was a great dancer, he could move well, all these things that I didn't have. But after the bad years with him, I decided the marriage went wrong because my husband could not understand the cultural stuff. I thought that being black, not exactly Chinese, that he would understand."

The marriages of people who married within their own group were happy only slightly more often than those of people who married outside. But, like Shirley, women with unhappy "mixed" marriages tend to think it was the difference in background that did them in.

Alice, in a cheerless relationship for many years, explains: "We got married in the city because my mother preferred that if I was getting married in a Catholic church, it wasn't in our hometown. She thought that might be a slap in the face of the Presbyterian church I'd gone to.

"My mother had two master's degrees, she came from a good family, she was an early feminist. And my father had been the Superintendent of Schools. He knew the Latin names for all the flora and fauna in the state. My husband's mother had an eighth-grade education and worked as a cleaning woman. She started a business in North Dakota and eventually made quite a bit of money—a lot more than we ever had—but certainly that was a very different background than the one I came from. Everything about our family was different—religion, education, grammar, and particularly other members of the family. I found that a shock. I don't think either of us took all that into account."

But there are very happy "mixed" marriages. Cecile, an engineer, is the agnostic daughter of a black Christian Scientist; her husband is the blue-eyed son of a big, ethnic, white Catholic family. "My husband's family went to church every Sunday, and he went to Catholic school until eighth grade. I never really had much respect for the organized religions that I've come across so I would question that in him, and that's how a lot of all kinds of discussions came about before we got married, in terms of what we expected from marriage and what we expected from each other. I think those conversations beforehand helped us be happy together."

Unhappily married women who stayed *within* their group blame bad temper, incompatibility, infidelity, abuse. Women in bad "mixed" marriages, after they mention the otherness factor, give the same reasons. Do some of these problems have ethnic roots? It would be an easy explanation of what went awry, but the theory does not hold up.

For example, one of the worst marriages I heard about involved a couple from exactly the same ethnic and religious background, where the husband frightfully abused his wife. In another instance, when a man physically and sexually mistreated a woman, she linked that behavior to his "alien" origins: "I'd gone to a girls school down here where you had your boys school next door, and you had your mixers where you met the right kind of people and did the things that you were expected to do. But when I got out of college, I began teaching in another state and I met my husband. My parents didn't say anything until we were getting divorced, but then they told me they never approved of him because of his arrogance. He was from Rhode Island, and up there it's a different personality, it's a different way of treating people that you're close to than here in the South. My present husband and I were both brought up in the same surroundings, the same people that love him love me too. He's from a good southern family, and I'm from a good southern family, and there weren't any mysteries about us. We both had kind of a bad break on the first one—his first wife was from down more toward the beach, and she was more of a self-centered person. My first husband was from the North and he had different ideas than we do about how you treat people."

Marrying Up

It was someone I interviewed who introduced me to the word "hypergamy," the custom of a woman marrying a man of higher social status. Though the sexes are reversed, that's what Lyndon Johnson meant when he characterized his marriage to Lady Bird as "marrying up."

> **There was little difference in the social standing of the majority of respondents and the men they chose to marry.**

A very few women married up in terms of money and education. The handful who married down seem to have done so deliberately to break out of their parents' homes. Their stories have the makings of potboiler novels, and their marriages all ended in divorce.

One Ph.D., from an upper-middle-class Jewish intellectual home, married an uneducated Maori. Another woman, Jeannette, is about five feet, seven inches tall, an African-American with round dark eyes and conservatively styled hair. She has the posture, speech, and self-confidence of the congressman's daughter she is: "When I was young, I wanted a large, football-player type. Years later it dawned on me: All that time pumping iron, your brain goes dead. They get big biceps but it stops right there.

"That image wasn't at all what I saw around me. I totally rejected the men I grew up with, the men I went to school with. I went to a Seven Sisters school, I was around people in the Ivy League, and I did not want those safe types. I wanted somebody who had a lot of street sense and didn't have so many of his edges smoothed off that he was no fun. My first husband was not at all like my father. He got his nails manicured, he wore big pinky rings, and his shirts were unbuttoned down to his navel. I finally woke up and totally rejected all that foolishness, and I took the lesson to heart when I went into this present marriage."

To stay with the African-American community, historically there have been few career opportunities for black men in our society. That situation still holds for much of the population but it has changed for the middle class, as Hope, forty-nine, explains: "My mother has a degree in biology, and my stepfather did too. My own father was a waiter, but in the black culture that was not necessarily an issue in those days. It was after the Depression, and his father, who was the town physician, died before he could finish high school. And so, even though my father had been headed for a career, he wound up being the breadwinner for his family. But times have changed. I can't imagine being married to someone who didn't have success in his career. That's terrible, and I feel elitist and snobbish and all of that, but it's important to me. If I'm already married to somebody and his career falls apart, that's entirely different. Of course I would stay married. But as far as getting involved with somebody who doesn't look like he's on any kind of track, no. It has to do with money, it has to do with prestige, it has to do with class. My family's professional, so I would just expect the person that I marry to be as well."

FALLING IN LOVE

Most of the women say they were in love with the men they chose to marry.

They were not describing a pallid or rational feeling, but it wasn't only sexual passion either. Like philosophers and song-writers, they were trying to fine-tune a description of the infusion of affectionate passion lovers feel for each other.

For a handful of women it was love at first sight as Amy, a recently married scientist, describes: "I fell in love with my husband right away, very quickly, faster than he fell in love with me. I couldn't help myself, I was crazy. Sometimes, when he was supposed to come over and then couldn't make it, I'd still be awake at 2:00 A.M. and I would call and yell at him. It was selfish and horrible but I just knew that I wanted him."

There are women for whom the process of falling in love was gradual, as it was for Cecile, married four years: "We started out just getting to know each other as friends for almost six months before we had our first date. I was the engineer on a big job across the street from where he worked, and we'd have lunch together almost every day. That was such a major thing, that we became friends. I got to know him as him, not as boyfriend or lover, just this person as this person."

And some women resisted. Helen, the daughter of an alcoholic father, did not marry until she was thirty-six: "By that time in my life I had gotten very adept at dodging men. I was so tired of the whole scene, I thought it was such a waste of time, I'd rather stay home and read a book. But when I met my husband he was absolutely persistent. He just kept calling me, kept writing me, kept asking me out. I always made some excuse. Then one day when I turned him down, he said, 'I have an idea. Why don't you pick a night when you don't have any plans and we'll go out?' We went out to dinner and had a wonderful time, and it went very fast after that, very intuitively. That intuitive stuff was falling in love. There's a part of it that is so irrational. Sometimes I think that it's purely olfactory. He's a great guy but, really, I had to marry him because of some way he smells, some weirdo thing."

> **Most of the women say that they could not have married or been happy thereafter without being in love. They feel you need the "stored electricity" to draw upon when difficulties arise, as they inevitably do.**

One woman talked about an engagement she broke off: "I don't know, I just looked at him one day and thought, I'm not in love. Whatever it is, it's just got to be there."

And from a Baltimore woman in a marriage with a fair number of highs and lows comes this clear statement: "I think it's important to be in love. I wouldn't choose for myself a pragmatic marriage, one that was based only on mutual help or convenience or companionship. I need something that has a current, a passion that draws you to this person. You are challenged at so many points in your marriage that you need to be sort of shot out of a cannon to ever get anywhere."

Not everybody who was in love went on to live happily ever after. A handful of women believe they might have been better off if love had not clouded their judgment. But there's another side:

Not one woman had a happy marriage who was not in love when she walked down the aisle.

We've heard Natalie explain marrying at nineteen for the security of going from her parents' home to her husband's. Now divorced, Natalie explains: "When we finally decided to do it, it was wonderful, I had achieved this important thing, I had an engagement ring. But the truth is, I was madly in love with the idea of being married, not with him. I was probably madly in love with him for a few weeks, not much more than that."

Though the majority of women were in love with the men they married, they did not marry only for that reason. Emily, forty-one, from a liberal southern family, makes the distinction: "All through high school there was always somebody I was in love with. But, though getting married was definitely in my expectations, I never expected to marry one of those boys. The school I went to was a hotbed of racists, and I felt very separated from them. I knew that they probably wouldn't go to college and they'd probably get married right away. That just wasn't what I wanted."

And something more subtle was going on: For many women, "suitability" was a prerequisite for falling in love. Helen believes that her attraction to her husband had to do with something intuitive, what she half seriously calls his smell. But she adds: "I felt that he was a wonderful package—great guy, strong, sensitive, and handsome, smart, has his own successful business, I'm wildly in love. Boy, what a luckout!"

Martha, whose parents introduced her to the promising lawyer she married, says: "Looking back, I think the qualities he had were part of it. They went hand in hand and contributed to being in love. If somebody didn't have those qualities, I wouldn't be able to fall in love."

Some of these "suitable" lovers made good husbands, some did not. The crucial difference was the way suitability was judged. In certain cases women used irrelevant standards or those of the people around them: "He was handsome and a great athlete"; or "Our parents thought we'd make a good match"; or "He was a very eligible man."

But when the judgment of a husband candidate is linked to a concept of the kind life you want, you stand a good chance of getting what you need—as Jane, at nineteen, so plainly did: "I could see that ideologically this man had the same ideas I did on what family is about."

....

There's a certain amount of insensitivity in summarizing in this fashion the outcome of choosing a particular man to marry. No one warned Erica when she was twenty-three that her adored, adoring, and provident husband could sicken and die, leaving her with ten children to raise. No one told Doris that her husband would have a lingering disease that stressed the family to its limits and was also passed on to her daughter. It would have been hard even for a person with a lot more experience than Camille had, in the days when premarital sex was taboo, to understand that a loving comrade could turn out to be an impotent husband. And to look at it from the opposite direction, only one woman made a hasty, "blind" marriage and had the great good luck to have it turn out fine.

Chance can play a dramatic part in the outcome of marriage choices. But for only a few respondents was Fate rather than Reason the determining factor. Mostly, picking the man with whom you have the best chance of a good marriage involves picturing the life you want and then measuring the candidate against that backdrop to see whether he fits in.

5

THE SEXUAL
COMPONENT

arly in these conversations, thanks largely to the
openness of the respondents, I began to see striking
patterns in the place of sexuality in marriage and in
how that derives from girlhood expectations. Some of these
patterns are related to generation; others occur among women
of all ages:

- Because of what they expected from marriage, many of the
  older women married for sex.* Almost none of the younger
  women did.
- Good sex is a bond between the older women and their husbands, but they also use it to avoid confronting emotional
  problems.
- The younger women almost never have sex when they're
  angry. They talk more with their husbands about issues
  between them, but they rarely experience the healing potential of nonverbal sexuality.
- Many more of the women believe that they have happy marriages than that they have rewarding sex lives.

---

* I'm using the term "sex" as the women did, meaning sexual intercourse, oral
sex, mutual masturbation, or other erotic caressing. They did not necessarily
mean orgasm—a woman might say, "We had sex but I didn't have an orgasm."
Nor did they mean, in one woman's distinction, "just cuddling and hugging."

- The sexual relationship is more likely to be used to measure the health of the marriage by older respondents than by younger ones.
- There are respondents in all generations who consider their own bodies the "playing field of sex," the couple's sexual home.
- The women want to be admired for the way they look in bed. They talk of wanting "to feel the male gaze" upon them.
- The women feel most aroused themselves when they are pursued. They maintain their girlhood belief that it is primarily the role of the male to initiate lovemaking.
- In good marriages and bad, a majority of the women report that their husbands rely on sex as a release from daily tension more than they do themselves.
- In almost every case in which the woman feels sexually needy, with an unresponsive husband, the marriage is in severe trouble. The reverse is not true.

SEXUAL EXPECTATIONS

We saw in the last chapter the society and family pressures that caused women to marry a particular man at a particular time. There was, however, another kind of pressure that pushed women to marry.

> Most of the women who married in the 1940s, 1950s, and early 1960s say that the desire for sexual experience was critical in their decision.* That was true for only a handful of those who married from the late 1960s on.

---

* It's hard to be specific about the age at which women were affected because, like global warming, the sexual revolution fell unevenly over the country. As a southerner pointed out, "The Sixties came to Mississippi a decade late"; and a born-again Christian, who married six years ago when she was thirty, said, "Up until my marriage I had exchanged only a few minor kisses that were very chaste."

The difference in motivation obviously was not a difference in physiology. Joyce, now in her fifties, had her first sexual experience with her husband just before they married. But this convent-educated woman remembers masturbating when she was very young. The accompanying fantasies about Jo of *Little Women* and her professor husband were romantic; obviously the book had not provided any sexual images of the couple.

Mona, thirty, had sexual intercourse for the first time at sixteen with a classmate at a suburban high school. Before that, she says, "I would make out with boys and not go much further than that, but then maybe come home and have a really hardcore fantasy and masturbate while I dreamed of somebody going down on me."

Girls masturbated in both periods but they had been provided with different material from which to draw their expectations. Joyce had not read the sexually explicit books and magazines, heard the language, nor seen the movies that were incorporated into Mona's sexual imaginings. As Kay, fifty-four, further explains: "The movies had a lot of influence in our lives, but they never really showed anything. They always ended with focusing on the outside of the bedroom window, the curtains flowing in the breeze. You never, ever saw 'it' happen and because of that we thought people didn't do that sort of thing before they were married. It wasn't acceptable in our world, and the movies didn't make it that way either. I never thought, We're going to do this or that when we're making love. You didn't even know about explicit then."

You Were Supposed to Wait

The older respondents grew up with the expectation that sex came along with marriage, that you had to marry if you wanted a reasonable sex life. Though not everyone waited until after the wedding, the majority of the older women only risked sexual intercourse when they thought marriage was a sure thing. And the men they knew agreed with them. The women believe that though their boyfriends may have been importuning, they nonetheless wanted to marry "respectable girls," those who didn't "sleep around."

In any case premarital sex was extremely difficult to manage: You might get caught; there were few places an unmarried couple could find privacy; your parents would find out; your family would be disgraced; you'd be considered damaged merchandise; no respectable man would want you. *And you might get pregnant.*

A woman of fifty-eight, describing why she did a lot of heavy petting but stopped short of intercourse, is only one of many women who mentioned the terror of pregnancy. Her explanation, though, is more subtle: "There was no such thing as a Pill, and there was an absolute fear of getting pregnant. I think it either kept me from having sex or it certainly was a handy device to use. Because I really wasn't doing that. I was of a mind that sex was very much part of a much more committed thing. I was not frivolous about it."

An artist of sixty-seven says, "Sex was important as a reason for getting married because you couldn't live together. There were good girls, the ones who held out, and there were the ones who weren't good. People were always talking about that. You couldn't help being influenced."

Another woman of this period, an Ohio actress who armed herself with a diaphragm before going on summer tour but did not finally have premarital intercourse, said, "Who knows what would have happened to me? I might have been ruined."

Now divorced, Kay is sure about why she married in the first place: "It wasn't right to have sex out of marriage, and my husband and I had a very torrid affair before we were married. So I *had* to marry him then, even though it wasn't that I was pregnant; it was because of all the sex."

Most premarital sex was with the men the women expected or hoped to marry. And the majority of them did, in fact, marry

those men. But even women who slept exclusively with their
fiancés worried: "If he got his way, would he cast you aside?
Would he decide not to marry you because the girl that he mar-
ries would have to be . . . a virgin?" Such women felt isolated.
They say things like: "Maybe it was just me"; or "I don't think
many other people did it." These statements are spoken with a
rising inflection. It's as if the women still want to find out if
other people behaved as they did.

I Was Ready

The result of these sanctions was that women were ready; their
bodies were pushing them to take the plunge: "We didn't have
sex until just before we married. We got married on the Fourth
of July and we had intercourse on Decoration Day. I wouldn't
have slept with him if we weren't going to get married, not then.
But the way things are now, wanting to the way I did, I probably
might."

Norma, a divorced southwesterner, said, "I think I married
my husband because I wanted to sleep with him. The logic was:
If you want to sleep with someone, you must be in love with
him; if you're in love with him, you should marry him."

Another woman, now in her sixties, told this story: "It got so
I couldn't think about anything else but what we'd done the
night before. Once I was sitting in class and I got this hot jolt of
what it felt like when he touched me a certain way. I didn't even
know I *had* that place before. I decided I'd better get married
and then get on with my life. Very logical, right?"

The Sexual Continuum

Though social attitudes had changed in the intervening years,
several women now in their fifties and sixties married for the
second time, too, with sex in mind. That was how their early
expectations had conditioned them to choose. Edith and her
second husband met about eight years ago, when she was about
fifty: "Here's a man who is a lot older, way up in his sixties when

we met, and we made love three times the first time we went to bed together. Around that time I would walk into a grocery store and think, Does anybody know what's going on in my life? Can they tell what's going on, the great sex? I thought about it today when I was driving down the valley. I thought, If he were not on jury duty today, I would call up and say, 'I really miss your skin.' And then I thought, God, I hope I never lose that, even if I get to be an old bag with wrinkles."

Furthermore, several of the older women who stayed married belie the old saw: "As it gets old, it gets cold." Lorraine, sixty-nine, married for forty-five years, says: "I was attracted to my husband physically but of course in those days we never did anything beforehand. The first couple of tries at intercourse it didn't seem so good—we were both inexperienced—and then it was fine and it's stayed that way. I thought it would be romantic at first and then the romance would probably stop. That's what I thought, but I find it isn't that way! It goes on and is even better in some ways."*

THE RESULTS OF MARRYING FOR SEX

As the younger women point out, wanting sex is not the most sensible motivation to marry; and how agitated your glands get in his presence may not be the best measure of whether a man will make a good life partner. Be that as it may, the effects of marrying for sex are mixed. Though some older respondents feel they made mistakes in marrying whom they did, few seem to regret the role of sexual desire in the decision. Instead, as the younger women deplore the repressiveness of earlier times, many of the older women say, "Where's the mystery now? The romance? The young people are missing a lot and their marriages aren't so great anyhow."

---

* Though she is too old to be in this study, a woman of seventy-six did say: "I'm just not interested in sex anymore and my girlfriends say the same thing. We're past that. It's the hormones, when they're gone you just don't care about it."

In the earlier generations, sex gave couples a powerful shove down the aisle and, from that beginning, it tended to stay near the center of the relationship. The level of desire, how many times a week you did it, who had an orgasm and how often, the timing of ecstasy—all these remained among the primary measurements used to calibrate how the marriage itself was doing.

> **For the older women, even when there were problems in other areas, good sex could be the bond that held the couple together, at least for a time.**

Physical closeness was considered a healing agent or an affirmation: "We may be fighting, but there must be something worth saving if we're still making love." And that statement gets to the heart of a generational difference.

> **Almost none of the younger women can conceive of "even touching" their husbands, no less making love, when they are angry. Many of the older women believe that the sex speaks for them—and especially for their husbands.**

The great majority of women now in their fifties or older married men who were masters of the traditional strong, silent style. The couple could not rely on open and emotionally probing conversations to solve problems as many younger people do. The result? Because they talk more, the younger couples don't rely on sex to communicate. But the older couples, through the nonverbal contact of lovemaking, may be affirming a strong connection between them.

Lisbeth, an animated, blonde and hip-looking sixty-seven-year-old Nebraskan who recently divorced after a long marriage, said: "There were times when we'd drift apart and then come together when sex seemed to be the glue. I think my husband

felt that sex would end the argument or end the big break—
penetration makes it okay, *penetration solves everything*. You
don't have to talk about what's wrong, you do it and then just
pick up and go on. And in a way there was something to it.
Whatever else was happening, we always slept close together, I
slept in his arms. I mean I didn't have forty terrible years. The
sex was a strong part of our marriage."

A good physical connection will not permanently cement a
bad relationship, however. When a marriage is consistently
problematic, the women, like Lisbeth, eventually give up on
the sexual component as they have given up on the marriage
itself. As a Bostonian of sixty-six put it, "Sometimes, when the
marriage was falling apart, we'd reach for each other and make
love because it was so sad that all this bad stuff was happening
when we had this bond together. The sex was the last thing
to go."

Several of the younger women seem shocked at the very
idea of ever making love when you're angry. I sometimes felt,
when I raised the question, that I was asking something inde-
cent. One West Coast woman of thirty-seven said: "If there are
problems in our relationship for either of us, we don't have an
interest in sex. When something happens I can't even go near
my husband, I get so angry."

A New Englander of the same age said: "Sometimes, after
we have a fight, way before anything is resolved at all, he'll reach
for me. He'll want to have sex for comfort. That's not my style,
that's not what I would do at all. Sex is far from my mind at that
point. It sounds like the fast route to making peace, but it certainly doesn't make peace with me, and it shouldn't with him
either."

The attitude of Louise, forty-one, was rare in this age group:
"There are times he's real quiet and doesn't say what's wrong. I
don't know if it's just that he doesn't want to communicate, or
maybe he's not sure what he's really feeling. I'd like him to talk
to me but, when he gets like that, a good night in bed together

and some good sex will usually open him up, start him back. It's like the tension will build up and he'll close himself off, and the sex is the way I get him to relax and be my friend again and talk to me."

There is in Louise's words a resonance of using "feminine wiles" to smooth things over. But let's posit a sensual paradise where both men and women talk about what's troubling them and also use the balm of lovemaking to help each other.

RATING MARITAL SEX

> About half the women feel they have happy marriages; fewer than a quarter have what they consider active and exciting sex lives. Of that group the largest proportion is now over sixty. Only a small minority is under forty.

What's going on? Why do so few women give sex a high mark, and why doesn't that more closely track their marital happiness? And what accounts for the age disparity?

The first answer is that many respondents don't consider the sexual component crucial to the success of the marriage. They seem to feel only a mild regret that their intimate lives aren't better. They think they can be happy without the earth moving. I heard this from women of all ages but most particularly from younger women.

Is this response just symptomatic of this stage of life, when work and children are so demanding? We'll look at the effects of work in chapter 7; as to kids, women of all ages say that immediately after their babies were born, they were emotionally and physically absorbed in them. But after that the frequency of lovemaking had little to do with the children, except that several older women tell stories about the sexual tonic to their marriages when the kids left home. They had more privacy and were old enough that they no longer worried about pregnancy. The women who expressed the most delight at this situation are those for whom sex had always been important.

Erica, for example, a widow of sixty-seven, had ten children: "When we got married, I wasn't afraid of sex, good Catholic girl though I was. I was enough in love with him that it seemed kind of natural, we both wanted to do it. Sex was a strong part of our marriage. I am a very sexual person, and we always had outward displays of affection. The children still tease about that. Some of their early memories, now that they have kids of their own, are of my husband coming up and kissing me while I was doing the dishes, or my sitting on his lap here in the chair."

SEX AND THE NEW MARRIAGE

It would be hard to overstate how different all this is for younger women. Few of them report a high level of sexual passion in their marriages.

I tried to figure this out with the people I saw, to understand whether what I was hearing made sense to them. The younger women weren't surprised; they married men to whom they were physically attracted but that is not the reason they married them. They think it would have been foolhardy to make a decision on that basis and then to go on to overemphasize the importance of sex in marriage. They say that lovemaking has a balanced place in their lives but that they value more other elements of their relationship with their husbands. They certainly don't envy what they regard as the hypocrisy of the social milieu in which their mothers lived.

Many of them volunteer that while they do go through periods when their responsibilities seem overwhelming, that's not the reason for the relatively low priority sex gets in their marriage. In fact, the low-keyed approach of women still in their twenties who do not yet have children would appear to confirm this. Lisa, twenty-nine, a midwestern lawyer married for less than a year and still childless, said: "When I was younger, there was a lot of pressure on people, and for me personally, to have a relationship where sex played a very important part. When it becomes overblown like that, the pressure is too much. I know I've settled down and my friends have too, to where sex is still important to a marriage but it doesn't have that overriding importance that it did. It's just another aspect."

The Pill

To account for the changes between their sexual attitudes and those of the women who came before them, younger respondents mention first the Pill.

> **The development of the birth-control pill, to a large extent, ended the paralyzing fear of unintended pregnancy. Post-Pill women expected more premarital sexual freedom than was available to their mothers because they thought they had better birth control.**

In fact, though it so influenced intimate lives, the Pill turned out to be a mixed blessing, one that perhaps changed expectations more than reality. As the Boston Women's Health Book Collective pointed out in 1970, a social side effect of the development of the Pill was that women became more vulnerable to sexual exploitation. A twenty-six-year-old describes how that worked in her life before she met her husband: "I was never forced to have sex, not physically, but there were times that I felt obligated. I really didn't want to do it but I had no good excuse; I couldn't even say pregnancy. Sometimes I felt that just doing it was easier because I didn't have too much reason not to, with the Pill."

To put it crudely, post-Pill women had lost their mothers' main alibi. At any rate, for many respondents the Pill was useful for a relatively short portion of their reproductive lives. They came to fear the health consequences of years of popping hor-mones and began the search for other methods—several of which posed unacceptable risks. Then, with the alarming spread of AIDS and other sexually transmitted diseases, when it became clear that condoms offered the best protection, unmar-ried women were pretty much back in their mothers' time, using birth control of practical and aesthetic complexities.*

Several of the women did get pregnant and did have abor-tions. A few married *because* they were pregnant. And a few younger women talk about the inhibiting effect of the pregnancy specter in their own lives. Zoë, thirty-six, recalls, "There was a scene engraved in my mind: Our church organist was a girl about my age and she got pregnant. She had to stand before the congregation, right at the front of the church, and apologize to everyone. It was *so* shameful I couldn't stand it, and I said to myself, 'That's *never* going to be me.'"

Despite these caveats there is no doubt that the safety the Pill promised was key to the irreversible changes that took place. More women had premarital sex than ever before. They slept with their husbands before they married them. They expected and got for themselves a freedom that was unprece-dented in our society.

The Sexual Revolution

And, of course, there was another, inextricably intertwined factor: the sexual revolution of the 1960s. Out of such influ-ences as post–World War II prosperity; the rebellion against society's restraints born of the civil rights and the anti–Vietnam movements; the emphasis on personal fulfillment; pub-lished research on sexual practice . . . a new climate arose that encouraged the free expression of sexuality. It had a powerful effect on women's lives.

---

* Things may change somewhat when the female condom is in wider use, since it apparently does not interfere with lovemaking.

The changes were swift and widespread. For example, we've heard respondents talk about the importance of the movies in shaping their expectations. Now, for the first time outside stag parties, films showed people undressed, in bed together, and clearly up to something—even if you couldn't quite see what. And nice girls were participating, apparently without punishment. They weren't ostracized, and the old warning that no man would want them because they were no longer virgins was patently untrue. If anything, their experience seemed to be a plus.

Books like *Our Bodies, Ourselves* and the work of Betty Friedan, Gloria Steinem, Robin Morgan, Kate Millett, Susan Brownmiller, and others urged women to take emotional and physical charge of their lives. Magazines offered sexual advice and encouraged readers to be adventurous. The result was that sexual expectations radically changed. Sex was no longer something you had to wait for. It was no longer confined to the marriage bed. The attitudes and experiences of many postrevolution women are like those that only men had been able even to imagine in previous generations.

For example, we heard Christine tell us in an earlier chapter that she never had a problem attracting boyfriends. She took this another step: "At one point I decided that I had a policy: I would only be involved in two-week relationships. That first two weeks is so wonderful, you're both faking it out, he's wining and dining, you're having a great time, you're on your best behavior. Then after that the real stuff comes out, you've got to deal with working things out. Forget it, have a good time and move on. So that's what I did for about a year. I started telling people up front, 'I've got to warn you, I only do two weeks.'"

Sara, thirty-six, is an academic at a small New England college. She has dark hair, expressive eyes, and a proudly carved Mediterranean face. With great intensity she described a love affair she, a self-proclaimed "nice Jewish doctor's daughter," had with a working-class Puerto Rican: "We had such a sexual hunger for each other that, though he was thirty-three and I was twenty-three, we both felt like it was the first relationship we'd ever had. It was a strange thing for me, like something an old-style man might do."

Sara's first husband was from a community in which she was doing research: "My husband had never been married before and he was four or five years younger than me. He was also a very virtuous, good boy, very respectful of women. He was a virgin when we met so, in a way, it was I who initiated him. It was a male-model relationship again."

Another woman talked of the sexual freedom she enjoyed after she divorced in her early thirties: "In between my two marriages I felt like somebody let out of school. I had spent a lot of time in a marriage that wasn't working very well while a lot of my friends were having affairs. I was really excited when I got out. I wanted to get my fill and have a lot of experiences and see what I could see. I felt like a fraternity boy or something."

THE EFFECTS OF FREEDOM

As the influence of the Pill and of the sexual revolution spread, sexual desire fell low on the list of reasons to marry. Though the younger women were interested in sex, marriage was no longer a prerequisite.

Rendezvous more convenient than car seats or back halls were available; many couples could sleep together and live together when they wanted to. In large segments of the population, premarital affairs were no longer scandalous. Though perhaps promiscuity was less widespread than the media portrayed, most of the women now in their twenties, thirties, forties, and early fifties had a fair amount of sexual experience before they married and, unlike the older women, slept with several partners.

With few exceptions the respondents who were virgins when they married are over fifty-five. Among women now in their forties, only a small number of southerners had no premarital intercourse. The only women now in their thirties who waited until marriage are born-again Christians, and one of those was sexually abused in her childhood. None of the women now in their twenties were virgins when they married.

It's Not the Center

....

Couples who have a sexual relationship before they marry get that over with; they don't rush into marriage because they can't wait to jump into bed. In fact, the initial sexual passion often has cooled by the time they marry.

....

And something else seems to follow. Because the subject is not so charged *before*, there seems to be less pressure to perform *after* the wedding, less need to keep track of how the sex life is measuring up. If passion takes its place as only one of several cords that hold the relationship together, other qualities may be more valued—as it may be undervalued.

Emily, forty-one, a journalist in a happy second marriage, says of her first marriage at twenty-three: "Sex wasn't a big thing in why any of my friends got married. Everybody already had done it in college. In a way that was better, it didn't put a disproportionate emphasis on sex afterward. It just settled into part of daily life. In my first marriage, I suppose if the sex had been better it would have helped but I think that we clashed so much about everything that sex wouldn't have been enough. It didn't count for much when we decided to get married, and it didn't count for much later on."

It was in the Northwest that I saw an intriguing example of this attitude. Daisy and her husband are both in their mid-twenties. It was seven in the evening when I got to their house. The air was so clear and the twilight so golden that, standing together in their garden, the couple looked like lovers in a fairy tale.

That impression was not incorrect. They are good-looking, they are in love, they are happy. But sex? Here's what Daisy says: "I don't think very many, if any, of my friends were virgins when they got married or even when they got out of school. But if I try to be truthful I'd have to say that the sex matters very little to my husband and me. I'm wondering if that's healthy after two years of marriage"—and here she laughed—"but it's really not important. We do so many other things together. We go for a walk every night after work for about an hour, and it's one time when you can really just relax and talk about whatever. I can really say that I don't think either one of us thinks about sex very much. It just happens when it happens, not that often."

Anne, twenty-nine, has been married for five years: "The sexual passion already has waned in my marriage compared to when we first met. In some ways it gets deeper in a more caring way and not as much of just the pure passion or lust type of thing. But I always say, if I could just bottle that up, what we used to have—I think back to when we'd just met—you need no sleep, you don't even eat. Oh, to be together making love is just so wonderful, I need nothing else in life. If I could bottle that!"

Amy, married for three years, has active sexual fantasies and sometimes considers the possibility of an extramarital affair. And yet she says that she and her husband seldom make love. In sharp contrast is her exuberant account of her teenage dreams: "I thought before I had sex, that once you have it, why would you do anything else? That it was going to be so great that it seemed inconceivable to me that people would bother doing anything else. Like why go to a movie? You could have sex. Why watch TV? You could have sex. Why read a book? I just imagined that you do the bare minimum to keep yourself alive and have sex the rest of the time."

For many of the older women such an early falling off of sexual excitement in a marriage would have been heartbreaking. As one such woman said, "Look, I have friends for companionship and a handyman to fix the sink. I earn a good living myself, thank you. If there's no sex with a husband, why be married?"

Yet, time and time again, the younger women use much the same language Maria did: "On a scale of one to ten, sex, I would say, gets a three. There are so many other things that I can't live without more than that. If something happened and we couldn't have sex anymore, I would stay exactly where I am. It seems kind of scary, because I'm only twenty-six, but there's so much more that I get from him that I couldn't get from anybody else."

Keeping Score

Something else may be at work: It may be that the younger women have a harder time than their mothers articulating what they want out of marriage. The older women had a brief check-list: They wanted their husbands to be good at the things men were supposed to be good at—making a living, making love, fixing the bathroom door. If you were lucky enough to have married such a man, you'd be well supported, well loved, and the house would be in good repair.

Now, as a thirtyish New York filmmaker said: "The roles are much more confused. It's harder to say what each person's supposed to be doing in the marriage and also what's supposed to constitute a good marriage. It's not so clear that any one thing, like who makes the living or how good the sex is, is central."

THE PLAYING FIELD OF SEX

We've been looking at differences between the generations in sexual expectations and experiences but respondents of all ages also share a number of important similarities. It is to those we will now turn.

> Many of the women see their own bodies as the playing field of sex, the geography on which love-making takes place. With this assessment of themselves, they tell us a great deal about the dynamic of their sexual relationships and expectations.

The women are not referring to using their appearance to tempt their husbands to make love to them. To understand the distinction, imagine hanging on the wall calendar art of a scantily clad and suggestively beckoning young woman. That's the classic picture of Woman, the Enticer. Now hang (it's imaginary, after all) the reclining Manet *Olympia* or a huge Rubens, breasts and belly set out before us. Those paintings present the woman's body as the scene of the sexual action.

Anne, a tall, fair woman in her twenties, is a former champion figure skater, now a partner in a burgeoning investment company. She bemoans the fact that because she has not been in competition for a few years, her body is not as toned as it used to be. When I asked about her husband she admitted that he also was out of shape, but then quickly dismissed the comment. It doesn't matter, she said, because "It doesn't seem like sex takes place in the man's body. I mean you take somebody in. It's about you."

Maria, also in her twenties, is about five feet eight inches tall, with a large frame and handsome features: "I feel that I don't make as much of an effort as I should in my appearance. He says he's happy with me and he surely behaves like he is, but I still feel I should be doing something more. It's hard to explain but what it is, is that you are the receptor, you are the bank or something like that. You owe it to the act of sex and to the person to be absolutely perfect—though I don't think that's possible, especially when we don't even know what perfect is. Movies, magazines, books definitely do it to us, where people are always airbrushed and lighted in such a way that they look perfect. It's not possible in real life but it's what I want to be."

Echoes of these words reverberated everywhere. Gloria, forty, has a responsible and highly visible job. With obvious pain, this attractive and energetic woman described what she imagines her husband must be thinking about her body: "I've gained so much weight since I was in my best shape. I try to lose it but I don't think I'm trying hard enough. If my husband would definitely say, 'I really want you to do this,' then maybe I would. I think deep down inside, he would like that. He's put on weight too, but that wasn't one of the reasons that attracted me to him as much as it did him to me. What attracted me to him was his personality and just the way he dealt with situations, where to him, I think the physical appearance was much more important. I would like to say that sex isn't only about us, isn't totally the woman's body, but then why do I worry about it so much? That it gets in the way?"

Unlike the men Gloria and Maria are married to, a few husbands do collude in their wives' insecurity about their bodies. A midwesterner says: "He married me for my looks but I didn't know that at the time. I thought he was looking for a nice home, salmon patties. All the years of our marriage, he only doled out pennies for me to buy the things we really needed but then he'd shell out thousands of dollars when he thought I should fly off to a plastic surgeon because according to him, I needed a tuck here and there."

The husbands of several respondents referred directly to the "turnoff" of their appearance. Such reactions at least temporarily confirm the women's fears: They are not doing their part, they are not providing a body that is an appropriate site of lovemaking. And the men add another log to the fire: They also blame their wives' appearance for their own lack of interest in sex.

At fifty, Wendy is a successful St. Louis entrepreneur. She is divorced; her children are grown. She's involved with a man who interests her, and she appears content in her new life, especially when she compares it to her former problems: "As my marriage was breaking up, he'd begun telling me I was a turnoff. Anyhow, whether it was cause or effect, I just didn't live up to his image. I think it was his problem. He was blaming me for his lack of libido, saying that he had to get drunk or smoke pot to psych himself up to have sex with me. Unfortunately at the time I bought into it; it's hard not to. And it was very destructive, very demeaning."

Adornment

In some relationships what the woman wears becomes another variation on the theme. Stella and her husband live in a small Baltimore apartment with two young children. Two evenings a week, after the kids are put to bed, the couple meets for sexual rendezvous: "I plan our dates every week. I have a trunkful of theatrical clothes. There's this unbelievably beautiful sea-mist green chiffon gown from the Twenties or Thirties. I thought it would look beautiful wet, so I planned a whole evening in the bathroom with the shower on.

"I recently went out of state on some business and when I talked to him on the phone, he said he'd like to buy me some lingerie. He'd narrowed it down to a Merry Widow and a lace nightgown. I told him I'd prefer the lace gown because I feel like I can do more with that. The Merry Widow you put on and your bottom half—well, if it's just left hanging out there exposed, what are you shooting for anyway? I told him that with a lace gown, you could do so many things. I sort of involved him in the fantasy over the phone of how you could wrap the lace gown around both of us, drape it in certain ways, how he could get under it too. . . . When I came home from my trip, the gown was hanging on the front door."

But at the same time she's setting the sexual scene on her own body, Stella, like many of the women, believes she is failing her husband: "When I gain weight I think he feels cheated from the experience of a woman's body, that I'm not being fair, that I have one to give and I'm withholding it somehow. When we're making love, I worry all the time about the way I look. It really has a tremendous effect on the kind of intimacy I'm willing to engage in, not only physically, but emotionally. If you feel you look awful, you're less likely to be free. You're embarrassed about taking your clothes off. And he complains about that, that

I'm hiding from him. He'll buy lingerie, and I don't want to put it on because I feel like I'm a poor imitation of what you're supposed to look like, so better none than that."

A New Englander, forty-nine, in a second marriage filled with work and kids and social service, remembers such feelings but has freed herself of them: "I think my appearance got in the way of my own sexual pleasure up until this year. I finally decided, the hell with it. I am almost fifty years old and I'm not going to look like I'm twenty because I'm not. This stomach is my stomach, it's three children and that's life, and that's too bad. But it's an issue for my husband. I know that he would love me to look the way I did when we got married. I'm not that much bigger, but the package has shifted a little bit. He would love me to still be able to wear a bikini or wear sexy things when we're in bed making love that I didn't even wear when I was thirty. I wouldn't be caught dead in them."

Paradoxically we hear echoes of this concept of the woman's body from people who *don't* worry about the way they look. Cornelia, sixty-six, said: "After my divorce, when I would start a new affair, I would think to myself, Wow, this guy's in for a big surprise. Wait till he sees what a great body I have." She didn't mention what he would look like when he got his clothes off.

> It isn't the man's obligation to look good in bed because his body isn't the designated location for the sexual act.

And even if we concentrate only on sexual attraction, the scales tilt wildly out of balance. Women are attracted to handsome men. They make comments about men with good bodies, "cute buns," and "great legs." Nevertheless no woman I spoke to ever said anything remotely like, "My husband looks so sexy, I can't keep my hands off him." Instead they convey that it is the woman's role to be attractive, the man's to be attracted. Stella's husband is five years younger than she is and apparently quite handsome. But when I asked her whether there are occasions, apart from their sexual dates, when she catches a glimpse of this good-looking man and wants to jump into bed with him, she answered rather crossly, "Of course not. That's what men do."

Barbara, forty-six, says she has an active and exciting sex life. A former tennis player who doesn't exercise much anymore, she says that though he himself is in terrific physical shape, her husband doesn't seem to notice her "flab" at all.

After the interview Barbara showed me an oil painting over the mantel in her front parlor. She described the long hours she secretly sat for the artist in order to surprise her husband on his birthday. "He loves it," she said. "It's the first thing he shows new people when they come to the house." The portrait is of a somewhat younger Barbara, hair still black, in deep décolletage. It is clear that her body is the couple's sexual home. Luckily that does not seem to trouble her, but the responsibility of providing and then maintaining that home causes other women great suffering.

Body Image

The culturally drawn image of the ideal female is powerful and pervasive. The image changes with the times; it is ruthlessly enforced and attentively observed (though perhaps out of the corner of the eye); and then it is internalized by many women as their personal standard.

Perhaps the most heartbreaking example of how a woman's real or imagined appearance influences her intimate life lies in the experience of Camille, a divorced fifty-six-year-old professor-painter at a prestigious women's college. Camille has deep blue eyes and an elfin, heart-shaped face but she seems self-conscious about her somewhat small and widely spaced teeth: "Before we were married, my husband and I were really good friends, we enjoyed each other's company a lot. It changed when the sexual part was put onto it. It was terrible at the beginning, sexually it was terrible. He was impotent. I hadn't known. I was a virgin when we married.

"We had only a few good sexual experiences in the eleven years we were married. Pretty much that sullied o'er the whole marriage. I definitely blamed myself for his lack of sexual performance. It caused me pain, but in a way I was accustomed to it, to feeling a failure with men—because of my appearance. He blamed me most for his sexual failure. He said he didn't like my looks but he didn't give an alternative recipe that he would like more."

When Camille was a child, her father would make "playful" fun of her nose; her husband blamed her appearance for his impotence; a later lover treated her dismissively. Camille says she now understands that her husband's problems in the marriage bed were not connected to her appearance. But she wept throughout the interview until, tears in my own eyes, I said, "Look, it's just a book. We don't have to talk about any of this. Pretend I just stopped by for a cup of tea."

Fat

Two young women meet at a church where they're both making wedding arrangements for the same Sunday in June. They meet again the following December, and one asks the other how her marriage is going. "Terrific," she says, "it's everything I dreamed of. And yours?"

"Terrible," the second woman replies. "He's an awful person, tight, angry all the time. I don't know why I didn't see any of it before. I've been suffering so much I've lost twenty pounds since the wedding."

"That's awful. Why don't you leave him?"

"Oh, I will," the unhappy wife answers. "I've only got five more pounds to go."

American women are obsessed with body fat, we know that. But fat is a painful and obsessive subject for reasons beyond how you're going to look in tights or a narrow black skirt. Equally important is fat in the bedroom. For that is when women are most vulnerable, when they come naked to their husbands with what they perceive as their shortcomings plainly in sight.

Christine dismissed a compliment I made about her good looks: "I guess my appearance has never been a problem for me. I was a pretty kid and I know I don't look forty—with my clothes on. Naked, it's another thing. My girlfriend and I were laughing about that, how after a good sexy time, you get out of bed and have to back out of the room so your sagging behind doesn't show."

The women well understand where their preoccupation with weight comes from. Just as they resent the culture's impact on their girlhood dreams, everyone who expressed anxiety about fat understood that the body shape she was trying to fit was unrealistic, media drawn, and unfair. But they have always *expected* of themselves measurements that coincide with "official" specifications. If they don't, the women feel shamed. Perhaps even worse, they don't feel sexually aroused themselves.

The women I spoke to do not want sex if they don't feel attractive. That, sadly, is what it comes down to.

Linda, thirty-seven, with an infant and a toddler, is about five feet two inches tall and weighs 170 pounds. The pain she feels about her weight is palpable: "I had more boyfriends during my junior high years than I did in high school because I had already gained weight by then and I wasn't as attractive. There was always this pressure to be like *Seventeen* magazine and *Ingenue* and wear those kinds of clothes.

"I weigh now the most ever. By now I should have lost what I gained with the baby but I was nursing and couldn't really diet. I can't go to the health club because I'm so overweight I'll look terrible. I think my husband still fantasizes about having a slender woman. The weight is an ongoing problem for both of us. He never wanted to marry a fat woman. Up to now it hadn't really hindered our sex life, but now it does—not because of him, because of me. I feel just gross and I want to hide my body from him. Because of that, I don't feel sexual. What if I never lose weight and always look this way?"

IT'S IN THE EYES

"I want to feel his gaze upon me"; "I want him to look into my eyes when we're making love." How often women said something to this effect! They weren't talking about what's come to be known as the phallic gaze, the male come-on, the sizing up of a potential sexual partner. It was more like love light, the intense, nonverbal signal of deep love you're supposed to see in the lover's eye.

> **The respondents want to be admired in bed. They want to see in their lover-husband's lingering gaze acknowledgment that their body is beautiful, that they've done their part.**

But they often say something further about the eyes: "When we're making love, I want him to look into my eyes."

> **The women want to be individuated: Look into my eyes and see that it is me you're making love to, not someone else, not some anonymous receptacle.**

A Connecticut woman in her thirties worries that she and her husband rarely make love. When I tried to pin the problem down, she said that she wants her husband to watch her carefully during lovemaking and to notice *her* response to *his* making love to her. She wants him "to look at me in a certain way and say, 'Oh, I see that feels good.'" She wants to "feel the male gaze upon me."

When they talked about the male gaze or about eye contact, it was common for women to refer back to their girlhood dreams. Linda said: "I had a lot of romantic fantasies when I was young but, sexually, I would dream about someone looking me in the eyes with love, really looking straight at me and loving me, having the courage to be intimate emotionally as well as physically. That's what excited me and it still does. That's when I know, when he looks at me and loves me through his eyes. It's hard for my husband to keep that contact at intimate times. I could swear he did when we were dating. Can men really do that? I don't know if I'm being unrealistic or just being a woman."

Another woman described her girlhood ideas: "When I would think about sex I didn't have a particular setting, but I did have a sense of two bodies holding each other and gazing into each other's eyes. When we get into our mood swings, I miss the way we used to look at each other. We would look in each other's eyes and we knew it was a romantic time, from the eyes."

Most women talked about the loving gaze in the past tense, as something they do not now have, and with the same tone of rueful longing they used to describe abandoned dreams.

THE SEXUAL DANCE

Respondents have a traditional view, deriving from girlhood expectations, of the roles of men and women in lovemaking.

Sara, thirty-six, says: "I have always expected of the men I've been with a certain kind of romantic come-on, and definitely I'm disappointed if I don't get that. With my first husband I had to invent it, and women shouldn't have to do that. They don't have to initiate, they have to look good and smell good. The woman has to appear available, and I'm good at indicating that I'm just going with the flow of whatever's going on. But it's the man's responsibility to make the romantic overtures. I'm a feminist, I'm liberated. I grew up in an era where there were no social constrictions hampering me. And yet there's this bottom line where I don't feel that it's quite as legitimate for me to be aggressive romantically and sexually as it is for a man. I don't feel shy about initiating but it's not as exciting if I do it."

Natalie, in her mid-fifties, says of her former marriage: "It wasn't all his responsibility, I certainly made my contribution to the absence of a good relationship. I wasn't very articulate about personal things. It's a funny thing—here I was externally, professionally, very articulate, very outspoken, but I never really spoke up about my sexual needs. I never said, 'I want, I need.' I kept sort of waiting for him to figure it out, and then I'd be upset because he wasn't figuring it out, and then I'd just get into a tighter and tighter emotional ghetto."

Ginger, a film producer, has straight, thick blonde hair, clean and regular features. About sexual roles, she says: "My husband and I are very good friends, we're equal partners and we're a good team, but sometimes I don't feel I'm a woman. I'm always struggling to assert myself as a professional, just because I'm female. Sometimes I wonder if I've become overly aggressive and lost the ability to sit back a bit and be adored. I'm trying to let go of being always the in-charge person. I think it's important to actually reestablishing the romance, where I was less in control and was more being swept off my feet. In the sexual dance, we do assume roles—it's politically totally incorrect to say this. I've always been aggressive in pursuing, I'm not someone waiting for the phone to ring. But I think there's a certain female quality that's been lost or relinquished in the sexual dance. Men should do the work of luring you and then you decide if you want to submit, not only sexually, but even emotionally and romantically, and whether you're going to respond with softness. I don't think women today have a lot of opportunity to be soft."

All three of these women are committed feminists yet, in matters sexual, they do not believe that the initiative is properly theirs. Ginger thinks she must relinquish in bed the qualities that have made her successful in the world. It's as if she must give up who she is—a powerful woman—for sex to be good. And despite their strength in other matters, such women believe, as Sara says, "It's the man's responsibility to make the romantic overtures."

> Many of the women, no matter what their demeanor outside the bedroom, take as a given that it is they who have to be persuaded. They see sex as something they dispense to importuning men: You petition, I decide whether to give. This deeply ingrained pattern almost ensures an imbalance of desire between the sexes, or, at any rate, perpetuates the myth that there is one.

If women think it is their role to respond yea or nay to sexual petitions, if that is what they see as the natural way the dance is choreographed even in marriage, it makes it hard for them to initiate sexual activity, to do the asking. It also blocks them from acknowledging sexual passion when they haven't first been asked. Such women don't feel aroused unless they are pursued.

> In all the age, ethnic, geographic, and professional groups, a majority of respondents rarely initiate sex. They rarely are excited by their husbands' appearance. They rarely feel aroused unless they are pursued. They need acknowledgment that their bodies are sensual before they can feel sensual themselves.

An elaboration of this theme was offered by a Pennsylvanian: "I planned my own first seduction when I was twenty-one—motel, nightgown and all, and I did all that stuff to set the scene and make it sexy before I got my husband. The truth is that there's less excitement in married sex. The chase is gone. Part of what made it exciting before was the sneaking around attached to it. And it was exciting because I was picking the people. I gave my body to the person I wanted to give it to, whereas in marriage it can become a duty, something you're duty-bound to do whether you want to or not. Women aren't in control anymore when they marry. We've lost control of our bodies, they're at the call of our husbands. When I'm the one who picks the time and place, I like it more. Then I don't have to give up my body, I have control of it."

If you feel at your husband's "call," then naturally you feel you've lost control of your body. But it's a puzzler if ever there was one: Maybe you feel you're at his call because he's almost always the one coming on, you're never asking *him* to grant *you* sexual favors. The negotiation is mostly from one direction, and the tyranny of tradition remains firmly fixed.

SEXUAL ABUSE

The expectations of girls who were sexually abused were dominated by the experience. Linda was a virgin until she married at twenty-nine: "When I was five a man molested me and my friend. He stuck his thumb in—and made us sit there. He told us he'd kill us both if we moved. I managed to talk myself away and ran and got my aunt. She got there just in time to see him strangling my friend and almost killing her. I don't think that stuff turned me off sex but it did make me hate and fear a certain type of man. And I'm not comfortable alone in the presence of men."

Hilda lost her mother when she was a child: "My father molested my sister and me when my mother died. He'd call me into his room and he'd hold me and rub himself on me and fondle me. I wasn't scared, but it was very unpleasant. When I was a girl I'd have daydreams and crushes and be sexually excited by the boys my age, but the sexual act seemed repulsive. I'd be always nervous about somebody losing control the way my father did. I think I had frigidity over a number of years because of it. Even after I married, I'd be very excited and we'd have sex, but it didn't really work. I'd always feel this sort of anger. My husband was very considerate, but still I felt I was being forced to do something I didn't want. That, I'm sure, comes back to the fact that in reality I was forced by my father. I feel that I've been damaged in that I can never comfortably go and say, 'Come on, let's do it.'"

It was not only childhood trauma that had an effect. Shirley feels that her former husband disregarded her feelings in bed, but another factor was also at play: "Before we got married, I was raped by a friend of his, and the way my boyfriend dealt with it was, 'I'm not going to let a woman get in between my friend and me. We're going to continue going over to his house.' I was so sheltered and so naive that I went with it. But after it happened, I went home and I was shaking, I was a total mess. I was probably in shock for two or three weeks. But if it happened last week, I would report the guy; I didn't report him because he was my husband's friend. Now I would make his life hell."

Miriam reports problems from the first week of her marriage: "My husband abused me sexually, always. I never got a night's sleep, I could never say no. If I said no he'd punish me in a variety of ways which I still can't talk about. I wouldn't dare talk to anyone about it except my mother and she said, 'Be patient, he'll change.' If we shared a room with the kids at a hotel, he still wanted to have intercourse, and if I said no he'd be mad at me and he'd ruin the vacation for everybody. If I got my period he'd get mad. This is what goes on in life, life is not the movies, women get their period. But I would have to have sex. He'd force me."

HE WANTS IT MORE

That women who were abused may hold back from sexual experiences is understandable. But even if we put that factor aside:

In good marriages and bad, a majority of respondents say that their husbands' sexual desire is stronger than theirs.

Though there are a few women in whose marriages the interest in lovemaking is fairly even, much more common is the attitude in this vivid description: "He's my age, forty-five. Now supposedly the books tell you that our sexual appetite is heightened at this period, and theirs diminishes. Well, it's the flip. If he could be an implant, he would, that's how close he wants to be. A lot of times, he wants to make love and I'm thinking, Well, God, that'll take an hour, and I'll have to shower again in the morning, and I know I have to leave here at six—I'm trying not to have quarrels about this because it's certainly nothing you should hate your husband for. But he's just consumed with it all the time, and more so because of how I act, how he doesn't know when he's going to get it, because I'll say, 'No, I'm too tired, let's do it in the morning, let's do it tonight.'

"It makes you very guilty, like, God, he does all the cooking, he does all this, and I can't even do my little wifely duties. And you tell yourself, I better do it, it's been three days. He's getting that look. I have these little thought balloons going off in my head that are the answers I'd really like to say, but then, out loud, I say the wifely thing.

"It's not that sex isn't important. If I were dating him and the sex weren't any good, I wouldn't have married him. It's still good when we do it, it's not like anything has dropped off. But, for me, in the scheme of things, it's good to know it's there and that it's good when you go for it, but it's not crucial."

Women report that despite their husbands' larger sexual appetites, they are "patient" with their reluctant wives.

Here's one example from Doris, sixty-nine: "The sex was something that we had to sort of work out. It took a long time for me to truly enjoy it. At the beginning I had the whole thing in my head of 'I don't want to get pregnant right away.' My husband was very, very patient with me. He wasn't demanding and he was gentle because he was a big guy. I could even laugh and have fun but it took a while. He was very, very patient."

Even in one notably egalitarian marriage of a thirty-seven-year-old: "Sexual attraction was very important when we first met. I couldn't be with somebody if it wasn't, but we've had to come to terms with some things. I suppose our biggest fight would be he would want more sex than I would. I know that he can't keep his hands off me, so I'm very flattered by that. But when I sort of complain, he's like, 'Well, wouldn't you rather it be like this than I never want to touch you?' When we had children, there was a period when I wasn't interested, and he was respectful of that particular situation. I know that even though his needs weren't satisfied as well as he would've liked them to be, he was understanding and patient."

The Macho Connection

Respondents raised another possibility: Perhaps the husband welcomes the opportunity to seem patient.

....

The apparent disparity in sexual desire in their own marriages seems to some women a sham. They believe both partners actually have about the same libido but that the men follow the pattern of "I ask, you turn me down" so as to feel macho.

....

In fact, these women say, their husbands *know* the timing is off when they ask. They're not particularly interested themselves—not right now, that is—and they know they will not be put to the test, so to speak.

Two women of forty-two, one on the East Coast, one on the West, articulate this theory. Helen says: "I think it's very much the same with my husband because if the baby's up at night I'm not the only one who doesn't sleep. He doesn't either, and he's just as tired. Sometimes I think he likes to take the stance of, it's me, his wife, who's not up for sex. But it's not. I make jokes about it. I say, 'I don't see you sitting up in bed with your black negligee either.'"

Carol says: "My husband makes a lot of noise about wanting to have more sex. My theory is that he's safe doing this because he knows we can't! Because it's always these strange times when he asks, when we're surrounded by these kids and it's totally impossible. He also does come on at times when it is possible, but I don't know, we've fallen into these roles, right now anyway, where he is this stud, he has the greater desire than I do."

FOR MEN IT'S A RELEASE

Respondents commonly use the same two words—"relief" and "release"—to explain why their husbands want sex more than they do.

> **These women believe that for their husbands, sex is a relief from daily tensions, a release from the outside world—as it is not for them.**

We know relatively little about what arouses women's sexual interest, and the people I talked to themselves rule out possibilities that come readily to mind. For example, many women work hard at their jobs and also carry basic responsibility for home and child care. But respondents feel that does not explain the imbalance in sexual enthusiasm. Their husbands are tired too, they say; some of them do their share at home.

The difference is that for the men, according to their wives, sex is helpful when they're tired and stressed. For the women it is not. One woman's explanation is that it takes her longer to become aroused than her husband. Perhaps, if she is tired to begin with, she can't stay the course and achieve orgasm and, therefore, the relief her husband finds.

But an important element in the question of "relief" harks back to where the invitation is coming from. If, as many women do, you see yourself as always being asked for sex, then it can feel like just another chore; the person asking can strike you as still one more person nagging at you for something. Would these same men plead fatigue if their wives were "always at them" for sex?

If the men are not often pressed for sex, it doesn't feel like a chore to them. It's something they are seeking to fill their own needs. Sexual intercourse may be a way to affirm that though things are going badly at the office, here, in bed, where their true measure can be taken, they are competent. It may be a way men can express mastery over someone else when they themselves have been mastered in the outside world. It may simply be that when things are going badly, when they're weary and sore, the tenderness of lovemaking is a balm.

The respondents themselves offer still another explanation:

Women of all ages say they need more emotional involvement than their husbands. They need "more transition from the workaday world to lovemaking." They want the romance, or the chase, or the admiring gaze before they get to the sex.

Sex is not a release from the world *unless* the scene has been set romantically, unless the women can prepare themselves for a shift in gears. Some of them, almost apologizing, say they think sex is "more natural" for their husbands because they don't require that conditions be just right. The women don't seem to be alluding here to sexual foreplay but rather to *psychological* preparation, to getting your head in a place where you want sex yourself and do not see it as still another duty, still another demand being made upon you.

Here are two of the many voices that illustrate this point of view, the first from a woman with a teenage son and an important career: "Almost all my friends' husbands seem to have tremendous sexual drive. The men are always demanding and the women mostly resent it. They're tired when they finish working and taking care of their children, their husbands are sexually demanding, then angry at the wives. It's not that the men aren't taking the responsibility for the kids and the work at home. They are, a lot of times. The problem is that we can't automatically make the transition from our work lives to being passionate, sensual people. Men don't need emotional preparation for sex; women do."

Carol, the West Coast caterer: "I don't think it's that we don't need the sex. Maybe it's a sort of holdover from Victorianism. For my husband this is a drug. He has a terrible day at work, he comes home and complains, 'Everything's awful, let's have sex.' Because this is the one thing that's going to make him feel good. Maybe just chemically or physiologically, that's the way it is for the men. For me it doesn't work like that, it's not a turn-on. If I've had a terrible day, I want to go to sleep. I want to be left alone. It can't just be a drug I take. It has to be a more romantic thing."

WHEN WOMEN ARE NEEDY

Among women who report that their husbands "want it more," there are many apparently happy marriages. However:

....

In every situation where the wife wanted sexual contact more often than her husband, it indicated a general malaise in the marriage.

....

The reality is so at odds with what they expected, these women are miserable. When they were girls, there were no models of a sexual relationship where a woman had more sexual desire than a man. No one expected that. We saw a few pages back the tragedy of an impotent husband. Sue Ellen, an Ohioan of forty-three, feels that her husband deliberately withholds sex as a matter of control—as men sometimes accuse their wives of doing: "With my husband before we got married sex was very different than afterward. I said to myself, Wait a minute, what's going on here? I thought women were the ones that did that, let themselves go and withdrew sexually after they got married. I think unconsciously it's a manipulative device, because if you make yourself unavailable and someone's always trying to cajole you, then it's a very passive-aggressive way to keep you hooked."

Ginger also described her distress at not being desired: "It's not until two weeks ago that I realized that though we still cuddle and can be very close, he'd withdrawn from me intimately, he was alienated sexually. I thought I was just managing to slide by without having sex with him but then I suddenly said, Don't be so self-centered about this. This man is having as many problems with you as you are with him on this issue. When I realized that, it was painful for me. He wasn't urging me to have sex, and that's what kept us totally comfortable. But it's been a year! That means he hasn't wanted me all that time."

Most of the time, Martha reports, her husband does not want to make love: "I'm never attracted to anyone else. I have sexual needs but they're connected with my own husband, not Paul Newman. My husband's got a lot of discontent in his life— his wife has gotten heavier, he's not happy with that, it interferes with his enjoyment of sex. I think he's not happy with himself. I would have to say that he's cruel about withholding sex because obviously I have sexual needs too, and they're not considered. But he'd probably answer that he wants the relationship to be more glamorous."

THE LUSTY WOMEN

There is a small band of respondents, several of them in their sixties, whom I came to call "the lusty women," those who highly value sexuality and in whose lives it plays an important part. It's hard to generalize about them but they do share a sense of humor about themselves. Earlier in this chapter we heard Amy's girlhood question about sex: "Once you have it, why would you do anything else?"

Erica, sixty-seven, says: "Maybe I wanted sex so much it's

my own fault I had all ten of those kids!" In her marriage Erica was made to feel a most desirable woman, and that probably fed her own sexual desires: "I remember we were in an airport in Boston one time, and this lady had a gorgeous fur coat on. I said, really just joking, 'Why don't you buy me a coat like that?' We were walking up the ramp and he answered me, 'Because you have such gorgeous legs. Why would you want a fur coat?' It wasn't like I really wanted the fur or that he didn't want to get it for me. It was just that he really did feel I was so gorgeous on my own, it would just be gilding the lily to get the coat."

Barbara, forty-six, says about the intimate life she and her husband share: "He's very good in bed. Very. In fact I've teased him, 'How do you know all this stuff, have you been reading magazines?' As an example, everything he does, he does quickly—except when he gets in bed, and then he's got all the time in the world. I laugh about people who have affairs on the side. I don't know how they have the time. I mean he is the most sexually ready person I can imagine. And he is probably more attracted to me today than the day he married me."

And from Cornelia, sixty-six: "When I was a kid, I thought about sex all the time, I was burning up with it. I'd sit on a bus and the place where my thigh was touching the man next to me would be on fire. When I thought about after I got married, I'd imagine we'd have sex all weekend, that we'd never get out of bed. I loved making love, and my husband and I did do it a lot. After I got divorced it stayed that way, there was always someone there. It's only in the last couple of years that I haven't had someone around to share that with. It's what I miss most."

Did their sexiness make them happy? The lusty women say that while they were making love they were joyful. But about a quarter of these women divorced. Though that's not a bad record given the overall national figures, still, in many cases, good sex was not enough to hold a problematic marriage together. Nor does a bad sexual relationship, on its own, shatter most marriages. Of course, the trick in that sentence is "on its own." The sexual component was part of a panoply of conditions that either nurtured or undermined the relationship.

In that sense, the women are right who say that the sexual component is not paramount but only one factor in the marriage. But the sexual relationship itself grows out of many factors: cultural expectations, ambivalence about women's bodies, the uneven and shifting power in marriage, and stubbornly persistent gender roles. Even so, the lusty women who praise the joys of making love seem to have something in their lives other people do not. And the really fortunate women are those who have managed to put sex in its place—and still to be excited about it. Because they are not imprisoned by expectations and because their husbands are supportive, the marriages of these women are enhanced by lovemaking.

6

CHILDREN:
BETTER THAN
ANY DREAM

t was children, not husbands, most of the women dreamed about when they were girls. They imagined kids in their minivans, kids at the dinner table, kids in their arms. They were confident that when the time came, they themselves would be cornucopias of motherhood, bestowing love and nurture within sheltering marriages. In this chapter we'll look at the way these expectations of maternity worked out in the lives of the women I saw.

WHEN AND HOW MANY?

With the exception of one woman in whose family there is mental illness, when they were girls, the respondents all expected to have children.*

About three-quarters of them did, and about half the remainder hope to in the future. Mirroring the national averages, the age

---

* I interviewed only women who at some point married; perhaps people with no interest in children are less motivated to marry or, at least, to marry during their childbearing years. No respondent made her first marriage past that age, nor did I interview anyone who was not married at the time of a child's birth.

CHILDREN: BETTER THAN ANY DREAM ~ 89

at which they have their first child has risen with the generations. Two children are most common, though there are a
couple of older women who have ten or more. A few children
died in early childhood, a few as adults. Some of the women
have had miscarriages or abortions, and some have never con-
ceived. Almost no one in her twenties has children yet, though
they all expect to.

BETTER THAN ANY DREAM

The world expects of women that they bear children, and they
expect it of themselves. They also expect children to make them
happy—and they are not disappointed.

....

**The respondents, whether or not they enjoyed the
daily routine, said they loved the experience of having
children.**

....

But children, not surprisingly, made profound changes in
their lives. Helen, a New Yorker with a busy career and a two-
year-old, says: "When I had my son I felt like one of the mother
gorillas on the PBS *Nature* shows, where the babies sort of cling
on. There's definitely something about having the baby and
nursing him that takes over your attention."

A virgin when she married at thirty-one, Stella became
pregnant quickly thereafter: "I felt overwhelmed. I couldn't
have my old identity anymore. There I was, Boom, bride!
Boom, mother! You were just on the duty side now—breast-
feeding, weight gain. I don't think people have a clue about
how their lives are going to change once they have a child. I
thought that marriage would be the great divide, but now I see
it's parenting."

Because they've heard such stories, still-childless younger
women worry about the future as Amy, the New England scientist, does: "I'm not pregnant and I don't know when I will be,
but it's more real now than it ever has been. We say things like,

'Our kids will be so cute, they'll have big brown eyes.' I sometimes wish I could go ten, fifteen years into the future and see
what's going on and say, 'Oh, things are okay, I don't have to
worry so much about what's going to happen to us if we do this
or that.' But things will change between my husband and me
when we have kids. It will stress the relationship because it will
stress everything in our lives. That's one of the reasons I'm so
frightened of having kids, because I'm afraid of giving up who I
am now."

In fact, with the birth of a child, the way women identify
themselves changes: "I had a picture in my head of my
orphaned baby every time I thought about doing some of the
crazy stuff, like rock climbing, I used to." They trade the sports
car for a sedan; buy clothes that can recover from a productive
infant burp; and give up rock climbing. Older women point out
that it wasn't until their children were grown that they "went
back to being eighteen" and became adventurous again.

Even with the Problems

There are problems that can make the task of raising a child
seem overwhelming; these include poverty, overwork, poor
housing, severe behavioral or physical disturbances. . . . We see
evidence every day of parents in all economic groups who
abuse or neglect children or who cannot cope with caring for
them.

I heard none of this from the women I talked to. One
reason is economic: Some people had trouble paying for education, orthodontia, expensive toys—but none of their children
went hungry or homeless; all the families managed to get help
for their own or their children's difficulties.

Though their lives change, though motherhood is often
physically arduous, economically stressful, and emotionally
trying, the women focus on the bright side, forgetting or dis-
missing the complexities as transient. The pleasure seems to
outweigh the pain. As one woman said:

CHILDREN: BETTER THAN ANY DREAM   91

....

"Having a baby is the one area of my life where the fantasy was not as good as the reality. They put that baby in your arms and, my God, the love is incredible."

....

Rita remembers: "I thought maybe at some point I might have kids but that was not my first priority when I was in my early twenties. It was a big shock to me when I got pregnant before we were married. This was not a planned pregnancy but the minute he was born, the minute I saw my son, I adored him. I thought, This is just too neat. This is great."

Norma says: "I don't regret taking so long to divorce and find out I was a lesbian. If I'd realized it earlier I might not have had kids and that would have been terrible. I feel real sorrow for people who were a couple of years behind me. Now they're in their fifties and desperately want a family, but it's too late."

Women in unhappy marriages tend to see the children as their compensation. Alice looks at all the years she has remained in the harsh climate of her marriage: "Sometimes I wonder whether I would have been better off staying single but the thing about never marrying at all is that it would be very hard to give up having children. Children enrich your life."

Even mothers who have had to cope with disability, illness, learning problems, emotional instability, rebelliousness, drinking, drugs—stubbornly struggle to set things right and put a good face on it. Miriam describes such a situation: "My son was born legally blind. I tried to divorce my husband when my boy was two and a half. The lawyers knew I was being abused physically and sexually but they told me to go home, that I would never get enough money to raise my daughter and keep my son out of a state school for the blind. So I stayed and I found out how to get him what he needed, and we did it. Now he sees almost perfectly. I can't imagine life without my children. If I never do anything else in my life—of course I hope I do—but if I don't, my children have satisfied something in me that could not be equaled. I could imagine being successful in other areas but nothing like raising these children."

Though it is hardly a "problem" in the same sense, a mid-westerner describes her reactions to her son's homosexuality: "My son is gay. At first it was hard because you don't want your child to be in a very difficult setting—I mean of all the ways to have to live in this world! You worry, What did I do wrong? If I had been a closer, more attentive parent . . . all those classic things. But at the same time you understand more and more what it is to be gay, and that it would have happened anyway, and you begin to see how you can behave yourself. I'm eternally grateful for this child. He's a delightful human being, absolutely wondrous."

A Life Without Kids

Considering their girlhood expectations and the pleasure women get from their children, it's no wonder that those who are now experiencing problems with fertility feel tremendous anxiety; or that virtually every woman who had an abortion regrets that she had to—despite her confidence that the decision was right for the time. Some childless women have had to come to terms with their regret: Jeannette, forty-five, says: "When I was a girl I dreamed of having lots and lots of kids. When I got married, I told everybody I was going to throw my birth-control pills in the ocean my wedding night. I had a child and I lost her at my baby shower. That night was the worst experience of my life. I'm really disappointed about not having kids but realistically it's not going to happen anymore. I have what I call rental children now, the children of friends. I'll take them for a weekend maybe, or out for a day. And you don't have to send them to college!"

There are several women without children who seem content but a woman of fifty-four who was married only briefly has had second thoughts: "I thought children would get in the way of my career because in those days you couldn't do both. And we knew from the beginning that the marriage was not right, so my husband was not eager. I actually got pregnant when we were breaking up but we didn't have the baby. It's just that I was so afraid that the child would be born with emotional problems like my sister and father had, terrible mood swings, everything short of suicide. There was no amniocentesis in those days. Sometimes I think I've missed something in life, there's a missed dimension. It's an experience you should have, the actual experience of conceiving and giving birth. I wish I'd had that—and the children themselves."

I'm a Wonderful Mother

The women expected to have children and they expected to be good mothers. In fact, they seem compelled to think of themselves that way.

The few who express doubts about the job they're doing talk about the circumstances: "I wish I'd been able to give them a less tense home." "I should spend more time with them." "A better father." And even these women protest that in the end it came out well—or will: "Like most parents, I wish I hadn't yelled, I wish I wasn't so hard. But my daughter keeps saying that she had a very happy childhood and I answer, 'Tell me, tell me. I'm happy to hear this.' I would feel devastated if they didn't have a happy childhood."

This woman would feel devastated because she loves her kids and wants them to have a good life. But there is another compelling reason.

The Children's Manager

If they did not do well at the job of raising children, women would feel that they had failed at the life-work they and society have expected of them since they were girls.

It's not the only work they do, it's not the only life they have. But for the women I talked to, the experience of having children is of central importance.

> Furthermore they consider child rearing their territory. Whatever their lack of assertiveness in other areas, however much participation they want from their husbands, the women want basic control of how the kids are raised.

Partly that's because they think they know how to do it best. But they also seem to consider the control theirs by right. There was a ready explanation in the past when gender roles were more narrowly defined. When they were denied a significant place in the outside world, women guarded jealously the one area where they could be boss and also could point to a major accomplishment—the wonderful children they raised.

But young women, despite their life outside the home, remain on guard. Those now in their thirties, with demanding careers, still want to be in charge of the children. They expect their husbands' participation but they want to set the tone for day-to-day decision making; like their mothers before them, they want to be the philosophical and practical director of their child's upbringing.

Ginger, for example, has no problem turning her year-old son over to a nanny during the day or leaving him home with his father while she goes off on a business trip. But who's in charge? "The basic responsibility is mine. My husband is great with the kid and very loving, they're bonded. But it works the same way with the house: I sometimes complain that my job is just as tough as his and I want more help. But then I go back to him and say, 'Excuse me, I'm wrong. The fact is, I like it run my way and if I want it run my way, I have to do it myself.' It's the same with our son. I'm responsible because I want it done my way."

Another woman puts a different spin on why she is the sole caregiver of two young children: "My husband's very nervous being alone with the kids. I fault myself for that because I used to make comments on his inadequacy so now he says he doesn't feel competent taking care of them. The result is I tend not to go anywhere or do stuff without the kids."

Who Takes Care of the Kids?

How do husbands feel about this arrangement? They seem to concede an implicit bargain:

You do most of the work of child rearing, you get to make most of the decisions. You can be important at home; I'll be important at work.

As we'll see in chapter 7, in all but a few families the husband's job takes priority. And when child care comes up, even when the wife earns more and has a more demanding career, it is usually her work that is judged expendable. This balance of duty and authority is what the women who married before the 1970s expected. The children would be the mother's to raise—with help from a loving, supporting, rule-enforcing, and judicious father. During the 1980s and, to a surprising extent, in the '90s, even in seemingly egalitarian marriages, the arrival of a child could upset the carefully stacked apple cart. Despite what women may have expected, despite the couple's discussions beforehand, many of the men assumed that, once they got pregnant, their wives would undertake—would *want*—most of the work of raising the children.

The bargain has not been easy to live with. Conceding control or doing more than you judge a fair share of the work provokes tension. And the lines have always blurred. For example, Daisy's father, now fifty-five, had his office at home and was at least as active a parent as her mother: "My dad would always take the phones off the hook when we came home in the afternoon and ask us how school was and take care of what we needed."

Though Edith, fifty-eight, did not expect parity, she chafed at the minimal role the children's father played: "My ex-husband's solution to everything was, hire somebody. Kids need a tutor, hire somebody; house needs straightening, hire somebody. What I really hated was when he wanted me to hire help for stuff that I wanted him to do, especially with the children. That would really make me crazy. Very early I figured out that I was the parent of the household, and there was nothing I could do about it. Asking him for help with the kids was like saying to someone who doesn't have an arm, Why don't you write with your right arm? They don't have one. The thing that I'm sorry about—and this is advice I would give to anybody who is in that kind of marriage—is just take hold of things. Don't pretend that the family is what the family is not. Don't pretend your kids have a different kind of father. Just do what needs doing, even though you might prefer that he was the kind of person who did it."

A few women and their husbands seem to have achieved a balance but even in certain families that look like they're sharing child care, there are resentments. For example, though Karen's husband had taken their school-age children on a camping trip the weekend I saw her, she pointed out: "It was I and not my husband who took time off from work after each child was born. I didn't nurse the children but it just somehow seemed that the person who needed to spend the most amount of time at home was me. I don't exactly resent it, but I want him to be aware that he's made many fewer adjustments to his job and his schedule than I have, even though he cared less about his professional development and career than I did."

The younger women and their husbands are subject to terrific stress. In general, couples need two incomes in order to have children in the first place. Both parents are working long hours and can't rely on a nearby extended family to pick up the slack. Many can't find or afford first-rate child care. For these reasons as well as because of changed expectations, many fathers do more of the work and take more of the responsibility for the children than was common in the past. Some fathers select the kids' clothes—hard to imagine a generation ago. But according to their wives, even these husbands do not assume that child care is equally theirs. Sometimes a woman would say that she knows fathers who are like that, but only a tiny percentage of the people I talked to claim such husbands for themselves.

HUSBAND AS FATHER, HUSBAND AS MATE

Whether or not they grew up in a home where a father was present, the women expected to provide one for their kids. However:

> They thought about the kind of dad they wanted for their children only slightly more often than they listed the qualifications for husband.

The exceptions were usually women who had difficult parents themselves. Maria, for example, says: "When I was young I dreamed about having kids. I guess that was easier to imagine than marriage because of my parents' terrible life and my father's drinking and drug abuse. Wanting to have children was one of the reasons I married my husband—I knew he was going to be a great parent because he's so loving and compassionate. When I met my husband and saw how he was with children, kind and strong, how they responded to him, that was insurance to me that it was going to be okay even though what I'd seen as a child was so bad."

Linda's list had a different emphasis: "I thought he was the right man to marry and have a family with, not because of the way he looks—he's not tall, he's not built, he's not a hunk, the things I wanted in a guy. But in my heart of hearts I knew this was the kind of man I should marry. He was responsible, steady, he had a strong Christian faith which was very important to me. At least, with people like that, you have a better chance because, before they do it, they're really going to think hard about divorce or about leaving you and your kids."

Grading Dad

Women have varying opinions of the way their husbands perform as fathers. Jane picked her husband carefully and also appreciates his qualities as a parent: "When they were babies my husband participated in taking care of them. And now, I get more angry at teenage stuff than he does. He'll say, 'Now remember, she's a teenager.' I'm more the disciplinarian. I can see they're lucky to have him around to balance things."

Stella is one of the few of the women whose husband stays home with the children. The consequences are complicated: "My husband's a very good father, better than I am a mother in a way. After all, there are so many times when they have scraped knees or questions, and I'm not there. I really struggle with that but the truth is, he'd rather take care of the children than have me do it and it's an ongoing issue between us."

Some of the women divorced husbands who they say were good fathers because the husband-wife relationship was so poor. But a southerner in a happy marriage wishes that when he deals with their adolescent kids, her husband would draw upon the apparently unending store of loving patience he shows for her. Instead she sees him "fly off the handle with the kids" and is surprised at such behavior in the man she so carefully chose to marry.

Only one man physically abused or grossly mistreated the children, so we can only speculate what the general impact on marriage would have been. There are several instances, however, where the women sorrowfully watch the men they chose as mate play the role of father. A woman with teenage children seems resigned to bide her time until the right moment to divorce. But when she talks about the children, there is despair in her voice: "He's not the kind of father I wanted my kids to have. It's been very painful for me because I feel like, How could I do this to them? He's okay with school projects and that stuff, but in terms of the fathering, someone who's able to give support, who's able to set limits calmly without being explosive, the emotional and spiritual involvement is just not there—as it's not there for me. God! As I talk about this and look at it, I start to feel such guilt that I've inflicted this terrible person on my children."

Joyce's husband constantly had affairs—with her friends, with the baby-sitter—but a midwestern judge awarded custody of their children to her husband because of his apparently stable, financially secure suburban life: "I always had a picture of him sitting there in that fancy house with his coffee mug full of vodka. They didn't realize he was a drunk at the time, and I didn't understand the severity of it. I don't know how I could have missed it! He once left my daughter, who was seven or eight, in charge of a two-year-old and a one-year-old. Can you imagine what it was like for me to hear that?"

Fighting Over the Kids

Children seemed to cause the most tension in the marriage when they are infants. Unless there are serious health or developmental problems, the stress usually lessened within the first year. In general, according to a study of two-career couples,* there appears to be no relationship between having a child and long-term psychological distress. There is also no long-term connection between the birth of a child and "marital-role quality." If existing marriage problems improve, then stress over parenting declines. If, apart from the kids, the couple's relationship worsens, stress about child rearing increases.

---

* Rosalind C. Barnett, Joseph H. Pleck, and Nancy L. Marshall, *The Relationship Between the Birth of a Child and Change in Psychological Distress in Dual Earner Couples* (Center for Research on Women, Wellesley College, 1992).

Much the same summary could be given for the notorious teenage years. The women who still have that period before them are apprehensive. Those who have passed through it say they and their husbands sometimes quarreled over how to handle adolescent problems. But they seem to feel that whatever was wrong with the kids—drugs, laziness, rebelliousness—there was no permanent damage to the marriage.

Which does not mean that everything went swimmingly or that the women don't think mistakes were made. Even in congenial marriages, couples may disagree on how to cope. Vivian, sixty-seven, who was happily married until her husband's recent death, described how he could not come to terms with one son's lack of motivation in high school and, against her wishes, eventually refused to help him. She believes that the boy might have had a more fulfilling life had they followed her instincts but she also gives a fair and dispassionate summary of her husband's reasoning.

We will soon hear Alice, sixty-two, describe how she used to be afraid of her husband. This marital relationship has never been good, and her husband's behavior to their son seems only to confirm Alice's judgment of him: "There was tension when my son was a teenager. His father just simply would become belligerent and rigid. I always worried about the temper. I think his sisters both feel that our son's spirit got broken."

Religious differences that otherwise don't matter may come to a head when there are children, especially over the rituals of circumcision and baptism. Ginger, a nonreligious Episcopalian, married an equally nonreligious Jew. Still, she says: "It always comes down to what we're going to do about kids. When my son was born, I definitely did not want him to be circumcised; circumcision to me is a joke. Against what everyone was saying— even my Anglican mother said he'd be better off in the locker room—I had convinced my husband not to have it done. But his father had a nervous breakdown, to the point where one day I finally said, 'Call a rabbi. I want to know why this is such a big deal. I want to know if he can be Jewish without a circumcised penis.' When the rabbi said no, I said, 'Fine, take it off now. If he chooses to be Jewish, I don't want to stand in his way. I'm not going to be the shiksa who's forever holding herself apart.' But it certainly was not what I wanted."

Stella is, like her husband, of Roman Catholic background, but they strongly disagree about baptism: "When our first child was born I wanted to have him baptized but my husband felt that a child should be old enough to be cognizant of the experience. We argued, we saw pastors, we saw priests. Neither of us felt we could compromise until he wasn't an infant anymore and the issue disappeared. But two years ago we had a child who was sick, with a strong possibility that she'd die unbaptized. My parents were very frightened; my father threatened to take the child himself and baptize her. The week before the surgery I told my husband that if the baby died without baptism, I didn't think our marriage would survive. I couldn't live with the regret I would feel. Finally, he decided I could go ahead and baptize the baby but that he couldn't participate. I wouldn't do that. What kind of marriage would that be? I said, 'I guess our child will have to live until she's old enough to know she's being baptized.' I think I had some intuition that the baby would be all right."

THE CHILDREN OR THE COUPLE?

Who, over time, in the opinion of the respondents, is at the center of the marriage, the children or the couple? I thought at first this question has a simple answer: It depends on where you are in your life—if the kids are small, they take a lot of time and energy, so naturally they're the focus; before they're born and when they later leave home, the couple is the center.

That turns out to be wrong. With the passing of infancy and unless the child has severe problems, parents of all ages and all life stages may or may not put the children at the center of the marriage.

> It does not seem to matter how time consuming child care is: People with help and without it, people with one child or twelve, give answers that vary according to the marital relationship. Of the women who say that the children are the focus of the family, only about a quarter have happy marriages. Where the couple is the focus, about half the marriages are happy.

Rachel, in her Mississippi front room, longs for the couple-centered marriage she saw in her childhood: "In my parents' house, there was no question that *they* were the center rather than the children, and that they loved each other. He would tell her she looked pretty and he never, ever, called her anything but 'Honey.' In fact, my brother and I only started calling her Mamma after we started school. I didn't feel shut out because all of us were included, but the parents just came first. And I still think it *is* the way things ought to be, the way I wish they were in my own marriage. It's what I expected but in my case, between my husband, my children, and my widowed father, I've felt literally like I was lying on the floor in three pieces."

It would be hard to imagine that the couple could remain the focus in a marriage like Vivian's, where there were twelve children. But she says: "With all the kids and all the time it took to raise them, my husband was always the most important one in my life. And I was in his. I don't think I ever felt torn between them, because it was a partnership. You see that so often in marriages that aren't doing so well, the children are the most important. I do not agree with that and I know my children appreciate that about their parents. My husband died last year and at the memorial service two of the kids read these beautiful poems they'd written about their father and about their parents' good marriage."

One explanation for what Vivian is describing may be that when the couple relationship is problematic, the children *are* the family. We heard Alice describe her husband's domineering behavior. She adds: "I used to be afraid of him too but eventually I just steeled myself and said this isn't going to bother me, what's important is the kids. When I was young, I always thought the marriage would be preeminent over the children, that the children would be kind of secondary. In fact it turned out the center of the marriage was very much the children."

> Women like this, who have remained with their husbands or who divorced only after the children left home, have not necessarily sacrificed for the sake of the kids. Instead the children provide both a distraction from marital problems and also the cement of the family life they value. Cooking dinner for them, attending their athletic events, making decisions about their health or their schooling—these constitute family life and may cover up or at least push aside acknowledgment that there's not much going on between husband and wife. In these marriages, whether they eventually break up or survive, it is as the parents of their children that the couple functions best together.

Camille, who long ago left the wasteland of her marriage, says: "My husband and I did manage throughout our marriage to go on loving our son and pretty clearly to let him know that whatever was going on between the two of us, we both loved him. Our son is in his twenties but occasionally, because we have a child, my husband and I still see each other. He has wanted to maintain the relationship because he still cares about our son."

Martha does not believe her husband and she will divorce but she does reflect on how the loss of family affects the marriage: "Our children essentially have grown and left. There is a certain pleasure—you don't have to call home and find out what the kids are doing. If you want to go to a four o'clock movie, wow, you can do that and eat dinner at six and come home at eight and not think about kids. Also because the children are launched reasonably successfully, that strengthens the marriage too. You can both feel good about them and how they're doing. On the other hand, there's a loss. There's less stuff in the marriage, less substance between us. There were lots of things that we used to do with the children we don't do anymore. On the one hand it's time-consuming, and on the other hand it embellishes your own relationship."

Women who had children soon after they married worry about something else: "It'll be interesting to see how our marriage does when the kids are grown since we really were never a couple, we got married and had our daughter so quickly. We've never had that time that people speak of, those first few years."

Having kids is a predetermined sentence—they're born, you raise them, they eventually leave home, and your attention can be concentrated elsewhere. However:

> In marriages where the focus was primarily on the kids it often did not shift to the couple when the children left home. Such people stayed closely involved in their adult children's lives and/or they became freshly committed to their work or to travel or other pursuits. They did not turn their attention to their spouses.

THE HAPPIEST TIME

Women say again and again that the happiest days of their lives are spent with their children. Without in any way devaluing that feeling, it may be appropriate to remember that since girlhood women have been "expecting"; they have made a powerful commitment to motherhood. Just as they need to think of themselves as good mothers, almost no matter what, they may need to gloss over any difficulties that would detract from their perception of the happiness children bring.

Never mind. I have engraved on my own heart a windy fall morning in a park above the Hudson River, the sun clear and bright, the sky somehow high for New York. The fallen leaves were dervishes in the wind, and the two small kids I had with me began spinning too, throwing leaves up into the restless air, laughing, drunk. Lying on the grass, the sound of them in my ears, leaves and breeze grazing my face, I said to myself: Remember this. This is happy.

Such feelings echo in the words of Doris, a Californian: "When we had the two kids? That was the happiest time in my life, when the children were really little and doing things together. I had the thought: If nothing else happens, this is nice. This is great for a life. I shouldn't have thought that, though."

Why not? Doris's daughter died several years ago of a swift and ruthless disease: "My husband and my daughter died within the same year. She was thirty-one. I could accept my husband getting sick but that my daughter—it was too much. Her illness was very, very short, just leaping. Every time I saw her, it was worse. The death of a child, that's the worst. It makes you different than other people. You think, What else could happen? Nothing that would measure up to this. I had a new roof on the house last year, and it was a total disaster. I came home from work, looked around at my destroyed kitchen, and I said, Well, it'll get cleaned up. After your child dies, nothing seems like too big a deal."

Do women who have lost children to ravaging disease regret having had them? Do they feel that they have subjected their beloved offspring to great pain by giving them life? It's a question I was not able to ask.

We should close this section with Vivian, whose children's memorial poems we've heard about. Vivian's large, ranch-style house was built about forty years ago in a development of the flatland beyond the mines that dominate this area of the country. The house is less than a mile past the unsightly and probably unhealthy mining pits that scar the landscape but, if you turn your back on the pits, there is from Vivian's front yard an exhilarating view of the mountains, snow covered even in August when I was there.

A crucifix hangs in the living room, as it does in many of the homes in these 50 percent Catholic towns. But the striking thing about the room is a wall of neatly aligned photographs, four across, three down, of Vivian's twelve children. Each portrait was taken at the high school senior prom. The boys are in bow ties and dinner jackets, the girls in formal dress. As we talked, Vivian would nod in each child's direction, referring to the wall as if to keep track of their names and birth order.

Not many people of recent generations have had twelve children, and no one I've ever known would want to. Nor do many of us, I suspect, have Vivian's apparently innate unflappability—she was the self-styled "undreamy child" we met earlier: "I never expected to have twelve children but I'm the kind of person that takes every day, and that's how it is. I did think, when I had the eighth, that was plenty. And then it happened, and, of course, I never considered abortion.

"My husband, especially at the beginning, would help a lot but as the years passed, his work took more time. But he was a very good father, very concerned about all of them. There were a lot of times we disagreed about raising the children, but we usually talked about it privately. The Sixties were a difficult time because the Church was changing, attitudes were changing, society had changed the way young people looked at things. Here they have all these choices that we didn't have to make. They don't know how to handle them, and it's very hard to give them advice. They felt we were in the Dark Ages—'That isn't the way it is now, Mother.' It took my husband a long time to realize that the drugs were out there but when he did, we agreed how to handle it, as much as a parent could. We were just lucky there weren't any real crises about it. The top ones, particularly, were born at a hard time. The boys had draft numbers and were opposed to Vietnam as I was opposed to the war. If one of my sons had gone to Canada or something, I would have supported him.

"I get along pretty well with all of them, I'm not really on the outs with any of them. I suppose I did a pretty good job but I'm sure, in retrospect, there are things I could have done better. Some days when they were small, you might feel like everybody's crying. Though I don't remember them, I'm sure there were days when you could have walked out, I'm sure there were. You don't remember everything, but I'm sure there were. I guess they weren't too important to me or I'd remember them."

....

As they forget the pain of childbirth, most of the women can't seem to remember for long the difficulties of raising children. Even those who are in the midst of a crisis say, in various versions, "It's hard right now but it will pass." Almost to a woman, the happiness they experience as mothers is much more important to them than the troubles. It is what they dreamed of.

7

HOW
WORK FITS IN

I recently came across a set of old-fashioned stereo-scope cards. Side by side on each card are two slightly different images of the same scene. When you look at them through a viewer, the photographs merge to make a lifelike three-dimensional picture.

When they were girls, the women had two different visions of the future. On one card children surround a loving mother, with a benign father looking on. On the other card there's an office or laboratory or courtroom, a busy woman at the center doing important work. The women had no mental stereoscope to position one image on the other. They dreamed of marriage and they dreamed of career but they almost never considered them together.

Describing this duality, a woman of forty-one says: "I assumed I'd be a teacher and be married. I never thought about who would take care of the children. It never entered my mind because I thought about a job and I thought about children, and it was two whole different games. When I played house, I wasn't a teacher, I was a mother. When I played school, I was a teacher."

It wasn't until they grew up and married that the women discovered that in reality the two lives were in the same picture. You couldn't consider career unless you settled child care. Your husband's attitude toward your work and that of family and society also had to be put in place. And the women I spoke to eventually found themselves evaluating their careers from still another perspective—asking not "How's my job?" but rather "How's my life?"

WORK DREAMS

More than half the respondents daydreamed about career, and almost without exception these women turned out to like their work. Sometimes the non-dreamers, pushed by circumstance, eventually found career satisfaction. But among the women who do not now have satisfying careers, no one spent time as a girl daydreaming about her future work.

We saw earlier that frequent daydreaming about marriage usually forecasts unhappiness. In the case of work, imagine yourself heading for a career and career satisfaction most often lies ahead of you. You may not know exactly what you're going to do; your fantasies may change or be tested by family, society, or financial complications; the essential thing is that you see yourself working successfully outside the home.

Only a few women had a sure idea of what they wanted to be when they grew up. Instead, they saw themselves in a variety of well-paying, interesting jobs. Erica, the widowed mother of ten children, is one of the few who had a specific early calling: "I always wanted to be a nurse. We had a program called *Clara Barton* on the radio that I listened to all the time. My mother had to buy a whole case of Dutch Cleanser and tear the labels off so I could get the uniform they were giving as a prize. I was named after my grandmother, who was a midwife, and she and I were very close. Though I never saw her deliver babies, I feel I got it from her."

Joyce, the Texan actress, says: "When I was young I was a bit of a klutz, and my mother thought that maybe I should take ballet lessons. The ballet class was closed, so I took dramatic lessons instead. I was four years old and I started learning little poems and being in recitals and in these amazing musical numbers. From then on I wanted to be an actress. I dreamed I would be famous, Katherine Cornell was my shining light. When I was about ten I got into the Civic Theater, and I remember the first play I was in and the smell of the grease paint. It was true—I did fall in love with it. I loved it, I'd found my place."

BEING FEMALE

Why didn't everyone dream of career? They were too busy dreaming of marriage. One woman of fifty-eight explains: "I got married when I was thirty. Before that I thought I had to appear as if I was available, rather than be a career woman. That's the message from childhood that I wasn't aware of, but that I was left with."

And from Linda: "When I was in college I lived in a house with four other women, all unmarried. You can imagine what the topic was in that basement—*men*, all the time. Nobody I knew thought just of having a career. I mean, I'm a painter, I love to paint, I'm blessed in that way. I didn't really have to work at it, I did it well, I started making money from my paintings very early on. Why didn't I concentrate on it when I was younger?"

Martha, whose marriage to a successful lawyer we've heard about, had been accepted by a graduate program but when the course was eliminated, she was encouraged to switch her application to Harvard, which for the first time was opening the business school to women: "I somehow didn't do it. I didn't think maybe I could ever get into the Harvard Business School. I don't know, I didn't apply. The word Harvard was pretty scary though it had felt secure to be in this women's program at Radcliffe. I never really knew what I wanted to do, had no clue. Once my father asked me what I was going to do, and I said, 'I don't know, I'll get a job.' That was the end of the discussion. The family never brought the topic up again. I guess they assumed I would get married or it just wasn't that important, I was a girl."

Family Expectations

> There were parents in all generations with tradi-tional ideas about what work was suitable for their daughters. These attitudes set restraints on what the women dared want for themselves.

Norma's family was politically progressive but, in practice: "My father had a master's from a prestigious university, but my mother would tell me I should go to college and not worry about my studies because I'd just find a husband and get married. In 1959 you were going to college to find a husband. I don't think my mother had a strong enough sense of self to be a feminist for herself *or* for me. Then again, I did meet my husband through my college roommate."

Though a few fathers told their daughters they "could do anything," others were less encouraging. The father of Edith, fifty-eight, was a newspaper editor: "I used to go up to my father's office sometimes and wish I could work there. I admired his work, but he made it clear that he thought women had a hard time in journalism, especially married women. He had a couple of good women friends who were journalists, but my doing that kind of work was not encouraged."

A public official talked his now forty-five-year-old daughter out of going into international law: "I was teaching at the college level and not really liking it, but I guess my father thought that was an okay profession for me. When I told him I wanted to study to go into international law, he said, 'Oh, you don't want to be a lawyer, it'll be harder to get married. People will be afraid of you.' He denies that now. No one in their right mind would admit to that in this day and age."

Louise, forty-one, is an elementary school teacher; her father is a circuit court judge; her mother did not work outside the home: "My mother encouraged me to do what I wanted to do, but when I was a little girl, it was sort of like, 'Are you going to be a nurse or are you going to be a teacher?' That was it. I don't really remember thinking of any other career for myself. I would play that I was a lawyer like my father. We'd have the courtrooms and the defendants and all that but, basically, I always knew I was going to be a teacher."

However, mothers were sending mixed messages. Though some of them downplayed career, they also urged their daughters to get the training to "take care of yourself in case anything happens"—and that "anything" meant a husband who left, or died, or failed at his task of supporting the family.

At thirty-two, Cecile has a smooth and bright complexion. With open features and grayish eyes, she carries herself with assurance despite the loose sweatshirt that, she says, "covers the fat." She and her husband live in a changing working-class New Jersey neighborhood in a newly remodeled apartment. The floors are beautifully polished, the furnishings simple and tasteful, the dining room table cluttered with the artifacts of Cecile's busy life—notices of meetings, political buttons, business letters.

Her relationship with her mother was stormy: "I don't think I should have been beaten the way I was, no child deserves that. I could do almost anything and she'd hit me. It really depended on her mood, that was one of the things that made it so frightening. You didn't know what would set it all off at any moment. So I figured out that it had nothing to do with my being good or bad, and I just did what I wanted to." Cecile got good scholarships and forged for herself a technical career in a field almost no African-American woman had ever worked in before. Whatever the problems between them, her mother's influence is clear: "My mother told my sisters and me that we have to get a college education, we must be able to support ourselves, because you don't know what's going to happen. She did want us to get married and to have a family, but always be able to support ourselves, because you never know when you'll have to."

Helen is a successful, well-paid publicist who also receives a great deal of recognition: "My father was an alcoholic and abusive, and, unfortunately, we were living in a state which had very conservative, restrictive divorce laws. They made it literally impossible for my mother to leave him without being destitute. She stayed much longer than she should have, waiting until I was through school. She was very committed to getting my sister and me educated because she always saw that as the ticket for us to escape what she'd had to put up with."

In Sandra's case the family provided the anti-model that set her dreaming of career. A petite, meticulously groomed blonde, Sandra admits to working hard on both her appearance and her style of life. Her apartment has a 180-degree view of the sea and is filled with the antique furniture and modern paintings she has collected: "I liked the romance of someday being with people who were cultured and sophisticated but it wasn't that I was going to marry one of them. I couldn't consider it. I even told the man I did marry, 'I've got too many problems. I can't bring you into them.' There was arguing all the time, the police were coming to the house because of what my sister might do in her manic state. My father was out of work and with his own mental problems. I always knew that the way out was to have a career. It wasn't money that was my notion of what I wanted when I was a girl. My notion was being right here where I am now, in this beautiful apartment on the water, surrounded by beautiful things, doing, and going. It was this kind of life I wanted, and I knew I had to get it on my own, with a career."

SOCIETY AND WOMEN'S WORK

....

Society tended to put a cap on girls' dreams of career.

....

Women are not unique in having trouble settling on a life work—it's not easy for men either. But the respondents have faced problems unique to their gender and to the role they play in marriage. No woman I talked to had dreams of being president of the United States—and no wonder! A forty-year-old showed me an occupational interest test she took in 1974. The scoring section at the end gives one set of recommendations for male students, another for female. The results indicate that a woman who had given these particular answers should become a psychiatric social worker, medical social worker, or psychologist. A man should become a psychiatrist, pediatrician, psychology professor, or journalist.

Rachel describes the effects of such attitudes on her own career ambitions: "I was right at the edge of a changing time for women, the difference between night and day at least in the South. Women who were only a year younger than I am, forty-four now instead of forty-five, began to do things like go to law school and get Ph.D.'s and not assume that all they were going to do is get married. I got straight A's in college and very high Graduate Record scores but the head of my department said, 'Well, you're just going to get married. You're not going to do anything with this anyhow.' So I fell into teaching not because I wanted to but because it was truly the only thing I knew. And unlike my parents who were teachers, I hated it and quit—and got married. I should have been an architect really. If I'd grown up any time but the Fifties I probably would have."

Alice, sixty-two, has sandy hair, regular features, and wears quiet suburban clothes. She lives in a large modern house set on an impeccably tended lawn that stretches down to a lake. She has spent her work life on the ground floor of that house as her husband's secretary: "When I was a young girl, I did very well academically, made Phi Beta Kappa. I went to Chapel Hill and I found out when I'd transferred to the business school that the professors didn't even like having women in their classes because, one thing, they couldn't tell dirty jokes like they were used to. You had to take partnership accounting to get course credit, so they allowed another coed and me to come into the class for just that section. We made the two highest grades, I was the top, and she was second in the whole class. But it isn't so clear-cut. The tendency, certainly among my women friends, was, 'Oh, well, you wouldn't want a bachelor of science anyway. A lady has to have a bachelor of arts.' There really just wasn't much encouragement for women to go on. I've regretted that in recent years, but I was having such a good time in college that I didn't feel deprived. We had seven boys to every girl, we thought we were in heaven. But lately when I look back and I see that even men I knew who were less accomplished academically have gone on and done extremely well—then I think, well, we were supposed to be an adjunct to a man, that's it."

Colliding Dreams

"I dreamed about marriage and family all the time. And I also had a confusing image of a corner office with a lot of books on the desk. But on the desk there was also a pipe and a man's hat was hanging on the hat rack. That was the confusion. Is that what I thought I was going to be? Or that there'd be a man sharing the office? Or my life?"

This woman of fifty-eight comes honestly by her confusion. If we look at the movies, for example, we see that there have always been conflicting messages about how women should conduct their lives. As Jeanine Basinger has pointed out,[*] even in the 1930s and 1940s, a film might show a

---

[*] Jeanine Basinger, *A Woman's View* (New York: Alfred A. Knopf, Inc., 1993).

reporter, or executive, or pilot who was better at what she did than most men. The moral of the movie, nevertheless, is that to be happy, she must devote her life not to the career she's so good at but to marriage. But young women did not walk out of theaters carrying only the fadeout—the heroine, apron askew, trying to scramble an egg. They also took away another image that affected their expectations: the glamorous career woman who could conquer adversity by her own wits and strength.

Still, there's little doubt that women now over about fifty saw marriage as the measure of success—though it was nicer also to have had an interesting career. Younger women are under pressure to have important and high-paying work—though you should also have a family. Both elements were present in both times but the emphasis and timing changed with the generations.

THE WORK–MARRIAGE REALITY

What did dreams of work come to? Most of the women have worked outside the home for at least a large part of their married lives. They are teachers and academics, social workers, nurses, psychologists, scientists, engineers, lawyers, entrepreneurs, secretaries, real estate agents, financial experts, writers, artists, corporate and nonprofit administrators. A few women have retired, only a small number are unemployed and looking for work. A very few women stayed at home for most of their lives.

Working Women

Women of all generations say that they encountered gender prejudice in their careers. The only exceptions were those in traditionally female occupations—teachers, nurses, dieticians.

So much has been written about this subject, it's enough to mention only one summary: A study by the Center for Women in Government* showed that about 70 percent of high-level jobs in state and local government were held by men. Black women held only about 5 percent of the best government jobs. Secretaries still make up the largest single group of working women.

But we must add to these statistics, the complication of family. Half the women in their thirties[†] and forties with school-age or younger children work full-time; a much smaller proportion of those in their fifties did so; and almost none of those in their sixties.

....

Because of a combination of problems in the workplace and their own conflicting feelings, the women have trouble reconciling career goals with the need to be a good mother.

....

Barbara, forty-six, is a southerner with the pride as well as the regrets common to women of her region: "I got a science degree, and when I graduated I thought that the only patriotic thing to do was to try to get a job in my home state. There was only one company interviewing for chemists at that time, so I took my little résumé, my transcripts, and that sort of stuff and went for the interview. My grades and my record were near the top, and the fellow was nice, but I got a letter shortly thereafter that said they were just terribly impressed with my credentials and so forth and so on, but that they didn't hire women because they would leave to have families. To show you how much times have changed, I didn't even know enough to be upset about it.

---

* Center for Women in Government, Rockefeller College of Public Affairs and Policy, 1990.

[†] Remember that some women in their thirties do not yet have children, and almost none in their twenties do.

But I did have the sense to think that if anybody ever says we've got brain drain, that our best and our brightest are leaving the state, I can say, 'Well, who's to blame?' I have three teenage children and I've worked most of the time, which they wouldn't have believed."

A twenty-eight-year-old scientist worries about getting pregnant: "I don't know how I'm going to finagle taking time off for babies. There's already enough of a problem with women not being taken seriously in science because 'they're just going to go and have babies anyway'—which I find very upsetting and totally ridiculous. What percentage of my total working life is that going to take up? And besides, after a baby's not nursing anymore, Mom and Dad are equal in what they can do. Men may feel that way but they don't have the same worry about 'What am I going to do when I have kids?' That's because a lot of them still have traditional wives who they know are going to take care of the whole thing, so they're going to be able to have their family and have their career in science and it's not going to be a problem. Whereas sometimes I feel like I'm going to have to do everything. And I really think it's unfair. I fantasize about being very successful. I want to be someone important, I want to be someone who's respected. On the other hand I don't know if I want to do what you have to, to achieve that status. So I have this conflict of really wanting to make a name for myself and yet really wanting to lead a normal life, with children."

How Hard Can It Be?

There are models in the women's own lives for how a family can function when the parents aren't home during the day. About the same number of mothers of respondents worked outside the home as did not. That's largely related to generation: Fewer than half the mothers of women now over forty worked; practically all the mothers of women in their twenties did.

There's a hidden zinger here: Traditional extended-family supports are no longer in place, even in ethnic groups that always relied on grandmothers to take up the slack. Only a very few women can call on family when they need help. And though, in general, women with working mothers assumed they would manage the way their mothers had, they didn't think out the details. They ended up in the same hard place: grandmothers now working or living far away, reliable child care hard to find and expensive.

Not all the mothers of the African-American women worked, but Hope's mother was a full-time biologist. Hope is forty-nine, with three kids, a demanding job, and a big, hard-to-maintain old house. She says: "It just never occurred to me to ask how I would manage a family and career, because my mother did it. All my friends work. We all came from families in which the mothers worked. Black women have always worked, we haven't had any choice." But Hope's grandmother was a strong presence in her life as a child. Her own children live too far away from their grandparents to get that kind of support.

The Father's Share

If the work of child care were equally divided, each parent would play an equal part in finding child care, monitoring school performance, arranging after-school activities, planning and preparing meals, staying home when a child is ill. They would each be left with the same amount of time and energy to devote to career. That seldom is the case.

Among the women I saw, only about a third of all fathers took such basic responsibility for the children. (Among women in their thirties, about half the fathers did so.) That meant that the work-family balance was a trick the women—rather than their husbands—had to learn.

The Families and Work Institute* recently put it dramatically: In the general population, when only the husband is working, the wife does 94 percent of the cooking and 93 percent of the child care. When both parents work, the wife does *80 percent* of the cooking and *70 percent* of the child care.

MY HUSBAND, MY WORK

> **Because, when they were girls, they rarely thought of work and marriage at the same time, the women didn't worry about how their nebulous husbands would mesh with their fantasy careers.**

Shirley, thirty-four, is an executive of a nonprofit organization: "My husband was very threatened by my work. The few times I brought him to business events with me, he would make me feel guilty because I didn't spend time with him. Now that I'm divorced, it's affected my dating in the sense of how some men approach me. I don't identify myself by my title and I try not to use it. If people really push me, I say, 'Well, I'm the EVP, executive vice president.' When they hear that, a few of them have disappeared. They're just not used to the idea of a woman traveling and doing that well."

Shirley should take that reaction as an early warning: If a man is uncomfortable with your career, that doesn't augur well for the marriage.

> **None of the marriages are happy where the husband doesn't value his wife's work. Where husbands are supportive, about twice as many marriages are happy as are not.**

---

* As cited in the *New York Times*, June 20, 1993.

When Edith's children reached adolescence, she gave up her nine-to-five job and started her own business: "The company is fine now but naturally it was slow getting started. One time my ex-husband referred to my work as 'my little job.' My little job! I mean, what a terrible thing to say."

Rachel works part-time in a prestigious job she loves: "Sometimes my job interferes with my work at home, and that annoys my husband because it gets in the way of his domestic bliss. It hasn't always been that way, but my attitude these days is: Tough. I think it would bother him if I had a full-time job I was very committed to. He says I would have to make a lot of money in our income bracket for it to be worth the changes in our life-style. I'd have to get more help with the yard work and more household help, and by the time you pay taxes out of it . . . But it annoys me when my husband resents my work. I think to myself, Well, I resent like hell when he plays golf two or three times a week."

Natalie went back to work after the children were in school: "As I moved fairly quickly into a career, my husband wasn't interested in what I was doing. I used to read his stuff religiously, he never read a single thing that I wrote or anything I was proud of."

On the other hand, there are husbands who push their wives. Martha's husband has told her he wishes she were "more interesting." She said bitterly: "It would be wonderful as far as he's concerned if I were to become the city's leading historian. I think he has fantasies about it—the ideal woman, you know, who can do it all."

Of her husband's reason for pushing her, Carol says: "Right now, he hates the uncertainty of the freelancing I'm doing. He would really like me to get a regular job and a regular income like I used to have. But my daughter is only two, and I don't want to be away long hours, day in and day out. He says he's supportive of my work but he makes it very difficult for me to travel even though I'm gone for a day, two days at the most. He makes me go through this routine: 'It's too much responsibility, so overwhelming.' When I'm gone, like most women, I take care of it pretty much, line up the baby-sitter, the meals. He doesn't have to do much, but he puts me through hell. He wants me to work, he really cares about the money I make, but . . ."

Barbara's husband is a staunch supporter of her work: "It's surprised me, because he came from the same sort of mama-at-home background I did. But I think he's just plain smart. He knew that for this marriage to work, feeding my passion for my work was important. And he's ensured that I could be the best that I could be. Once, when I was elected to the board of directors of a big national organization, I'd just had a baby, I was still nursing. And he said, 'I want you to go. Line up a nurse and take the baby with you.'"

Norma feels it was her husband who made her career possible: "When we got married, though we didn't talk about it, I assumed that I was going to have children and that I would stay home. It was my husband who really pushed me to start working. My career as a college professor, I have to credit him with because I would probably have ended up staying with the kids a lot longer and then had a not-very-good job. He really initiated it; he sat down and helped me do the résumé and sell myself. Though we didn't realize it at the time, without that I would have been in big trouble when we split up."

THE IMPACT OF FAMILY ON CAREER

A majority of the women believe that they would have done better in their careers if they had not had family responsibilities.

Here's a sampling of what they report:

A New England writer: "I feel like I work all the time, my life is parceled out in fifteen-minute increments, teaching at three or four places, and all these conferences, and editing manuscripts. I can't wait to stop. When the kids are grown, after I've paid for schools and education, I'm going to feel like I have a trust fund. I'll probably stop working so much on the outside stuff and do my own writing. Right now I feel like I haven't gotten started yet, like I'm ready to explode." (52)

A full-time homemaker: "I met my husband during a polio epidemic right after World War II. I was a physical therapist, and when I got my degree, it was with honors. We were in the midst of a terrible epidemic! My husband had just graduated from medical school and, like me, he was swept up in it. Those were exciting times because this was serious stuff, and we thought we were doing the right thing, helping people, working side by side. Now—oh!—now I have a regret that I didn't continue, but I couldn't go work for my husband's competition, in their office; and I didn't want to work for my husband; and he was at the hospital a lot of the time, so I couldn't work there, not in such a small town where I knew it would cause problems with him. It just never seemed possible, so I had to give it up. I missed the boat." (67)

A West Coast publicist: "My boyfriend and I discussed careers and children before we married and it was classic—'Of course you'll quit your job and you'll raise the children.' Even now, years after the divorce, it pains me to remember that he used to say things like, 'Women who insist on having strong careers are more like men than they are like women,' the intimation being that they're not all women. No wife of his was going to be like that, and his children weren't going to be brought up by strangers. I didn't like it but I went along with it. We both had the goal in those days to get an important job. He did, so I was able to transfer a lot of my ambition and admiration to his career. I sublimated mine, didn't need to focus on that all the time, I could focus on our glass being half full with his career, not half empty with mine." (54)

A lawyer: "I used to be in another firm, doing very well, but later my husband needed me to be on hand for the children, and I needed him to give me some flexibility. If I have to stay home when one of the kids is sick, he can see it's for his benefit too, not just taking away from the firm. Sometimes I think the arrangement is so convenient it keeps me from doing other things, though I've run for local office and been involved in politics. I came within three hundred votes of winning but, I don't know, politics is a terrible life with a family. And I worry about how he feels if I get a lot more publicity than he does. On the other hand, right now all I have is a pretty limited personal injury practice." (42)

A painter: "I've done two pieces on commissions this year but with a two-year-old and a three-week-old it's tough. I guess you have to keep the perspective that it's a very short time that you're on full-time with the kids. My reps are selling my stuff, but I don't have time to prepare for a show, or get more reps, or anything like that. You can't just leave your work behind, it's part of who you are. I believe things will work out, I do believe it, but I was crying the other day, saying, 'Does this mean I can't be an artist and a mother at the same time?'" (37)

A couple of women concede that it was not family responsibilities that kept them from career achievement but their own low expectations. Sue Ellen mentioned her three kids to explain her failure to find rewarding work but then she broke off, laughed a little, and said: "I have a fantasy that I would have done all sorts of great things if I hadn't married. Realistically, I probably would have drifted around in that sort of formless way that Sixties people did, and still do. Perhaps I would have drifted to some ashram somewhere, been kind of like a lost soul wandering around."

Though girlhood fantasies of career predict happiness on the job, there are several women who had no particular career dreams but were forced to work to help support their families. Almost all of them are glad it happened. Jane found it hard to leave her baby, even with her mother: "If we hadn't needed the money, I don't think I would have been unhappy when my daughter was very young, without working. But what I'm doing now and all the independence it's given me—I'm glad I did it. In retrospect maybe I would have been unhappy if I hadn't been forced to work."

BUT WILL IT MAKE ME HAPPY?

....

Though they think they might have achieved more, few of the women have lasting regrets about the impact of family on career.

....

They tend to hold their work up against their life to see whether the whole picture is enhanced or spoiled. And their judgment is not based exclusively on traditional criteria. The welfare of the family is important but it isn't the only thing women consider. Instead, they pose a question radical for the workplace, asking: But will it make me happy?

When I asked women what they would do if they were offered the job of president of their company or principal of their school, they'd respond with their own questions: Will it leave me enough time for my children? Will it make me a hard person? Will I have to spend too much time doing work I don't like? Will I have time to enjoy life? How will it affect my relationship with my husband?

An important explanation may be that, though it varies from family to family, as we will see in the next chapter, it is the husband who usually bears the primary economic responsibility. Men, therefore, may not have the luxury of asking themselves certain basic questions about work. They may not dare to; slogging along may be the safest course.

But for many of the women the old answers to the question How am I doing? seem too confining. They look at their situation in the round, scanning the field with peripheral vision to examine not only the question at hand but the terrain that surrounds it. Their solutions to problems can sound overly complicated, when in fact they may be more complete and practical for the complicated lives women lead.

There are many examples of such attitudes. An older fashion designer describes the course of her career: "I took three years off from work full-time and another two years part-time to be with my kids when they were small. Would I have gone farther if I hadn't? Maybe, but in my business the question always is, 'What have you done for me lately?' I'd still have to prove myself again next season, like I do now. Anyhow, who says you have to do the same thing all your life? It was a financial squeeze but maybe my kids are better off because I was home. I wouldn't have missed their first step and their first word. I learned to bake and I took Italian lessons. You'd have to be pretty dumb to regret that."

Anne, a twenty-nine-year-old financial adviser, is very ambitious: "Even when I was a girl, I assumed I'd work after I got married but a few years ago I began to think about the practical side much more seriously. I thought maybe I'd be a doctor, but you know what? It's not that I'm not up for the challenge, it's that I want to have a family, I want to be married. It's not that I don't want to work hard. I love my present job. I can't imagine leaving when I have a child. It's an all-women firm and we've made something out of nothing; we have great clients, it's growing. And because I have a partnership in an all-female firm, I have a lot of flexibility. My boss and I have talked about how I'm going to be able to have a kid: I can work part-time for a while, I can take time off, I can come in and breast-feed right there in my own office."

Anne had an offer from a large brokerage house that would double her salary. She turned it down because her current work atmosphere acknowledges and accommodates the family responsibilities she expects to have.

It isn't only children whom women factor into their career decisions. Gloria, forty, has no children but: "I think sometimes about what I would be doing if I wasn't married. I guess I would really immerse myself in this field more than what I am and I think I'd go further. Being married, I've learned not to take things home from work. When I did that, it was causing problems in my marriage. But my husband's my biggest supporter. My boss is talking about retiring and my husband says, 'Why don't you get her job?' I can't do that. It's a lot more work; a lot of her outside time is spent in the field. But she's a widow; you can't be married and have that job. It requires a lot of personal time, and it would be bad for the marriage."

If we go one step further and put family aside, women still use a wide-angle lens to view their work. The day we talked, Helen, the successful publicist, was dressed in New York summer black, an unusually cut dress that makes the best of her neat blonde good looks. Though her husband chooses her clothes and other things in their lives that require a good visual sense, Helen's independent spirit is clear from the feisty way she navigates her daily life and approaches her work: "My career took off fast partly because I was a slave. I was so thrilled that somebody gave me a job and paid me: This is great; they're going to let me work all night, I'm so excited! Now that that stage is over, lots of times I think it would be wonderful not to work anymore but it doesn't have anything to do with the pull of family. It's just that I've worked for twenty years and I feel like, what do I want to do with the next twenty years? I just don't see work as everything. It's important to me, I enjoy it a lot, but it's business. I've invested our money so either my husband or I could leave if we want to, but his personal drive is much more intermingled in his business. I'm less emotionally attached. I make people a priority over my work. I don't think twice about getting up and leaving a meeting if something's wrong. My two-year-old dislocated his elbow a couple of months ago, and I got in a cab and ran down to the pediatrician. She popped it back in, and I went back to running the meeting. But it's not just my son. It's important to say that I would be like that with lots of people—my mother, or a close friend. It's just that the job's not my central concern."

When Barbara had to evaluate a career change, she took into account a variety of questions: "I went back for my M.B.A. degree but on the job I have here, they didn't give me a cup of coffee or the time of day for having achieved that objective. The placement counselors at the university were lining up these interviews, saying that with my science background and this M.B.A., I could do a lot. Visions of grandeur were popping up in my head of all these wonderful jobs I could get other places. My husband said, 'If you want to take a job with some company doing your new-found things and you would have to move, I am willing to look for another job, I am willing to move. The decision is yours.'

"I had to really, really think about that. What I finally decided was that even if I found the world's greatest job paying whatever, we probably would not improve our standard of living very much. Plus, in this town we're already established. We have the right friends, and we get invited to the right parties. Anywhere else we would have to start from scratch. Plus, when scientific experiments are done, you never change but one variable at a time, because then, if it doesn't work, you don't know what caused it. I told my husband: 'If we move, I've got a new job, you've got a new job, the kids've got new schools, and all of a sudden our marriage doesn't seem so swooft. If things in your life aren't right, you immediately say, 'Well, I need to go and be married to somebody else so my life won't be like this.' Because your marriage sort of describes who you are and what you're doing. And so I said it's not worth it and here we've stayed."

We've heard Amy express her fears about the impact on her career of having a baby. She also sees another side: "Scientists have extraordinarily messed up priorities. They think you have to make science into a religion and that it has to be the shining light and guiding purpose of your whole entire existence and being. I'm sorry, but it's not. It's something I enjoy doing and I do it well but my family and my friends are very important to me, and I like to do other things, not just my work."

....

Do such examples make it sound as if these women lack ambition or commitment to their work? In fact, a majority of them are involved in what they do and want to do it well. But they also want the pieces of their lives to fit together. That's different from "wanting it all": Most of the women feel they've already made career compromises for family. The result they're looking for is a rewarding life.

8

MONEY MATTERS

I should worry, I should care,
I should marry a millionaire.
He should die and I should cry
And I should marry another guy.

ive hundred years ago, when she was a girl, my mother jumped rope to that rhyme. It apparently had no impact at all on her choice of husband, and it was not even faintly evoked by the women I interviewed. Most of them insisted that they hardly thought about money when they were girls. And then they'd go on to describe the married life they'd envisioned—the car, the big house, the kids' lessons, the travel.

As Anne expressed it: "I've always wanted to be able to have the life I had when I was a kid. I dreamed of living on a lake in a nice house, being able to ski and to teach my kids to play tennis, to have a fun family and do the kind of stuff we did. I still have those visions, not because they're expensive, but because they're my dreams."

When they were young, women imagined a family life at least as comfortable as their parents'. Vivian's expectations, for example, sound modest but the life-style she's describing, when applied to her own family of twelve children, took some doing: "Before I got married, I always told my mother I hoped for as comfortable a life, really for the same life-style that I had as a little girl. I didn't want to be rich like a lot of my friends wanted to have so much more than they had when they were children, wanting this, this, and this. That never was important to me."

Several women who watched their parents struggle financially took that as an object lesson, an anti-model. They say things like, "I didn't want to have to watch every penny like my mother did." Or, "We all had to work too hard to pay for extras." A few such women set out to make money themselves; others, though they may not have verbalized it, seem to have factored money into their choice of husband.

RICH MAN, POOR MAN

Miriam, fifty-four, says that "in her day" she was one of the prettiest girls in the city. Her heavy, straight red hair and slightly blurring starlet features offer convincing evidence of that description. Now she speaks like a person in recovery from a long, abusive marriage and a divorce that left her financially comfortable but cut off from her "country club friends." Miriam's husband was a much older, wealthy man: "I didn't think too much about money until my teenage years, when my mother began complaining about how little we had and what a hardship it was. It terrified me that I might have a life like my mother's economically—not that we were so poor, but because she always talked about people who were rich. That's what gave me this image of it, of having money. I sure didn't want to be like my family but I didn't know how to get there on my own, I had no way of doing it on my own."

Of course, it's hard to imagine anyone saying flat out, "I married for money," but some of the women came close. When she explained why she stayed so long with her husband, one woman also cast light on her premarital thinking: "How could I have left him? Look at my baby, all the expensive special care he needed, how could I? I couldn't work, I couldn't earn any money. What could I do, just count on my looks again? Find another husband, because I was still cute?"

Another woman hated the only work she was trained to do: "I was afraid of supporting myself, I think that may have played some part in my deciding to get married. I was in love but the financial considerations were important. My husband was a doctor and would always make a good living, and maybe I wanted the security of marrying someone who was going to be successful." The echo of her words hung in the air as she began to talk again: "I don't mean I wanted to be rich. That wasn't it at all. In my house—my parents' house—security meant just being comfortable." She stopped again and nodded. "I guess, since money is security, it's hard to separate the two. I'd have to admit that."

Did they do the arithmetic and reject people whose balance sheet showed a shortfall? Not explicitly, but:

....

Subtle evaluations often were used to sift out men who were poor risks for providing the married life the women expected.

....

We heard Martha say she wouldn't have fallen in love with someone who wasn't eligible, and that included being able to earn a living. Women who married men whose careers had not yet jelled say they were confident that would soon happen. Others say that money wasn't a crucial qualification but that they "wouldn't want to marry a slob who couldn't take care of himself." They didn't care about a large income but would not want to be married to someone "with no self-respect."

Kay, who turned down a rich suitor, said: "I wouldn't have married someone I thought wasn't going to do well, who couldn't provide me with what my parents had provided me with. I wasn't after money. Obviously, if I had been, I would have married the wealthy young man I was going with. But it never occurred to me that I would not be comfortable. Probably, now that I think about it, I was assuming I'd go from my father's house, where he took care of me, to my husband's house, where he'd take care of me."

Ginger feels that she didn't weigh money in her choice of husband but it plays a part in her definition of marital roles: "I lived with a guy for years and I supported us but finally I just couldn't deal with it. I realized I was the man in that family, and it was not a role I liked. I'm still friends with him but I would say it couldn't have worked out in the long run."

Donna is married to a wealthy man: "I knew I had to marry somebody who had traveled and was intelligent. Those were the things that mattered to me, not money. In fact, there was a man I wanted to marry that didn't have any money. He was sweet, he was artistic, I'd come home and there was my dinner on the table and tulips in my bathroom. I would have married him but I just didn't think he had guts, and not having money was an example of it. He'd say, 'Oh, I want to buy a new car,' and wait a year before he bought it."

Reacting to what they considered their mothers' unfair pressure on their fathers, certain women seem to have tried to discount economic questions in choosing a husband: "I think I was consciously looking for someone who would not take care of me, in the sense, bizarre to say this, of providing a lot of money. Maybe because I was afraid of what that would all mean in terms of selling out, prostituting yourself. I had to do the opposite of what my mother said, that I should marry someone rich, not like my father."

However, only one woman consciously chose a man she knew had a limited financial future. At sixty-five Hilda is a successful Chicago artist whose house is filled with paintings and with her husband's sculpture. There's a wonderful table he made of a burled slab of wood, photographs everywhere of children and grandchildren, and an atmosphere of easy warmth: "I just knew I was going to be a career woman. I was not going to stay home and take care of the house and babies. That ruined a lot of romances for me. I would always make these speeches about how men and women should pitch in and do housework together. When I met my husband, I made my same speech, and he took my hand and said, 'Where have you been? I've been looking for you all my life!' He was making fun of me, really, but actually it's worked out, because I've been supporting him most of our lives, and he's done his share with the child raising."

This couple's money comes from Hilda's hard work, not from wealth she brought to the marriage. Not one woman I interviewed had more money than her husband at the time she married. Some of them eventually earn more or inherit enough to redress the imbalance, but a rich girl marrying a poor boy? Among the people I saw, that did not happen.

PAYING FOR THE DREAMS

You can't discuss financial expectations or realities without taking into account the surrounding economy. Money plays a different role in a Depression-baby marriage than in a union of baby boomers; monetary questions are more urgent when times are bad; local customs affect the way individual families relate to money. A couple of women in Los Angeles, for example, mentioned that the high salaries in the film industry made their own average middle-class family incomes seem pitifully small. When I got to a town in Montana and commented on how close together the houses were, it was explained that the mining company that had run the town wanted everyone, miners and executives alike, to be able to walk to work. That's how mansions and cottages ended up in such cozy democracy.

Almost everyone I spoke to in that town had a parent or grandparent who had been killed in a mine accident or died from silicosis. Conditions like these have a powerful influence, as Erica found: "There's a different mentality here from Wisconsin where I grew up. Wisconsin Germans are very conservative, we save money for the rainy day. Here, people spend the money as fast as they make it because when the bell rang on the hill it was somebody's husband died in the mine. So you lived for today. That was hard for me to get used to. Sometimes we didn't have any money and yet we went to the fanciest place to eat. Even though my husband was a professional, there wasn't always the money because there were strikes here and there were months that he didn't get paid. We always had enough to eat, but you know, like Easter shoes for the kids or things like that, we might not have."

Aside from such local differences, there are strong patterns in women's economic expectations. Take a ruler and draw a line diagonally from the bottom right corner of this page to the top left. That diagram would plot the connection between your generation and what portion of family income you expected to contribute.

> **Virtually all the women in their twenties, and two-thirds of those in their thirties, expected to contribute about as much as their husbands to family finances. That was true of half the women in their forties, and of virtually none in their fifties and sixties.**

Lorraine, sixty-nine, is a New England dietician: "I didn't really know what my husband was going to do when we got married, he was in graduate school. I just had faith that he would be a good breadwinner. I thought I would work after I got married but not after I had children. And I never did conceive that my earnings would be necessary for the family to get along. I was a little bit shocked at first when that came up. Now I'm glad because once the children left, I already had this good job. But at the beginning, I did resent it."

Lorraine was shocked that her earnings would be *necessary* to the family. Women of her generation expected that you might work for extras but they were not accustomed to the idea that their husbands actually needed help with what was their responsibility—to support the family. In another instance, Lisbeth, about the same age and far across the country, points out that her mother would do fine seamstress work at home: "My father felt she was working too hard because she'd stay up late, and it wasn't that they needed the money. This might be a little hint that she was working so that she could have some of her own money. I mean she kept the money she made and then if I wanted something, clothes or just fun, we could always do that."

Not one woman in any group expected to be the sole breadwinner after she married.

Even women who anticipated sharing economic responsibility did not imagine that their husbands would make no contribution at all. Stella, thirty-six, whose husband stays home with the children, says: "I thought quitting his job and spending full-time at his writing would be only a temporary thing but that's how we've ended up, with his taking care of the children and me being the only income earner. I never had that in mind when I was a girl. If I could have looked ahead I would have thought that it was peculiar."

Who Supports the Family?

In the chapter on children we saw that fathers consider child care the primary responsibility of their wives, though they may participate to varying degrees. Because their wives have a strong need to be good mothers, they do more of the work involved as part of a silent bargain to maintain control of how the children are raised. When we look at money we see the mirror image.

The majority of the women believe that it is primarily their husbands' responsibility to support the family, though their help may be needed. They want their husbands to be good providers; that is what they have always expected. In return, they may relinquish or allow themselves to be excluded from economic control.

These attitudes prevail across the generations, even among the women who contribute equally. They also prevail in all ethnic groups. For example, while they were growing up—though not necessarily in their own families—African-American respondents saw middle-class women forced by the economics of racism to support their children single-handedly. Still, the black women I talked to married men they were confident would earn a good living. Their financial expectations were the same as those of respondents in other groups except that, in the older generations, black women accepted that their participation might be essential to pay the cost of family life.

One African-American, forty, said: "I wouldn't want to marry someone who didn't have his stuff together about earning a living, and I always thought I'd do a lot better than my parents economically. My husband was in a business that was booming for a long time but the market has pretty much collapsed and he's really been struggling. So I'm earning a lot more than he does. The ironic thing is that I always knew him as somebody who did very well."

Who Earns More?

> Often women do not assume primary financial responsibility because they feel they can't earn as much as their husbands.

The statistics confirm their perception. Women earn 77 percent of what men do in identical jobs. Professions in which women predominate—teaching, social work—are low paid. And though the gap between women's pay and men's has been narrowing, that's only partly because women's wages have risen. As important is that men's wages have dropped. It's not that women's income is leaping up the ladder; the ladder itself is being lopped off.

Among the women I saw, about two-thirds of the husbands earn more than their wives. Fewer than a quarter of the wives earn more than their husbands; the rest earn about the same. But in addition to these numbers, we have to consider the financial prospects women anticipate for themselves. Sara says: "If I examine it, I see that I assume my husband will contribute more than I do only because he makes more. I've always known that either I'd be supporting myself with a meager few dollars a year or else I would be part of a couple and I would contribute what I could. I have a lot of desire to earn a big salary, I really do, but I doubt it will happen. I don't have the drive. I mean, people who are those academic hotshots are the equivalent of a senator, they really worked very hard and they wanted it very badly. I'd like the money but my life isn't oriented that way. I'm never going to make a lot of money."

Some of the high-salaried "hotshots" to whom Sara refers are women on the faculty of her own New England college. It was not uncommon for respondents to limit their own monetary expectations. "I have to say that I would never have been able to quit my job as a lawyer without my husband—both emotionally *and* financially. My income's dropped substantially so that, at this point in our lives, he makes more than I do though up till now, I made more. My husband is anxious to get his work life to the point where he can spend more time with me and with our kids when we have them, but he'd never feel free to do what I did—walk away."

That reaction prevails even when there's economic parity. Helen and her husband have savings enough to give them flexibility but: "I'm open to stopping what I do anytime. But even though we earn about the same, my husband doesn't feel free to change his career because he does feel he's the main bread-winner."

Unlike their husbands, who usually do not feel free to do so, the women seem to be asking the same question about money that they ask about work: Will it make me happy? For example, when I offered to wave my wand and double a woman's salary, she said: "If I had to choose between working for lots of money, fourteen hours a day, versus fun: I would choose fun. Even if my kids were on their own, I'd probably pick fun."

THE BY-PRODUCTS OF ECONOMICS

What's the impact on marriage of the economic equation? Let's begin with Helen, whose income is the same as her husband's: "I find it such a useful thing in all regards, not just economically but the psychology—that you're responsible for yourself, that you're capable of taking care of yourself. It just changes you fundamentally, it gives you courage and confidence, and it makes you happy. Our incomes are about the same. It really does even the scales out a lot, and it doesn't let you use money as an excuse. Everything's even. It was even when we went in and, with some ups and downs, it's stayed pretty comparable. Neither one of us ever can say 'I do more,' or 'I have to work harder.' We both have incredibly demanding jobs, and we both bring as much to the family in terms of value, so we both need to share in child care and the household. It just seems very straightforward. I don't know, money can do weird things. If a million dollars landed, I don't know . . . "

Another woman compares the situation in her first marriage to the financial parity she now has. Louise has the slim, carefully tended good looks of many southern women. Her nails are manicured; her dark hair is styled much like the early Farrah Fawcett's; she wears gold bracelets and rings with her snug jeans and sparkling white shirt. In her early forties, Louise teaches third grade and talks warmly of her students, as she is openly affectionate with her own children. She says: "I never knew what my first husband made as a doctor until we were divorced, and it was a lot more than I suspected. I thought about my present husband's earnings before we married, and I realized that we would be making about the same amount of money, that it would be a joint thing. But now I like that. I was happy that it would be about the same, that we would be equal. I didn't have that before."

Several women believe their husbands are resentful if they have the lower income, as Natalie describes: "When I went back to work, I moved fairly quickly to a point where, depending on when he was getting his next raise, there'd be times when I'd be making more money than he was. And it was kind of, 'Oh, isn't this cute?' I suspect it was something other than 'cute' for him. For me, it was glorious, wonderful. Never having had the dominant career, I thought it was terrific, I was bringing in the bigger paycheck. Maybe I shouldn't be guessing what was on his mind, but he's macho enough to have felt very much, 'Oh, I'm very proud of her,' with the clenched teeth meaning, 'I hate it.'"

You'd need a sketch of a Cheshire cat grin to get the flavor of Amy's description of her family's earning potential: "Five years from now I will probably make a lot more than my husband, and secretly I think it's great. He's really good at what he does, and he gets a lot of good feedback. But I will be very pleased to be earning more money—not that it will give me more power in the relationship—it's more of me flying in the face of conventional attitudes."

The younger women, in particular, can be uncomfortable if they must turn to their husbands for full support. Cecile, thirty-two, is going through a hard patch because of the recent decline in new construction: "Before the layoff I was an engineer earning a very good salary. I've always worked, I've always earned money. I feel a little bothered now about being dependent economically, and I've told my husband I wouldn't be happy living off his salary. I earned more than he did, always. It didn't bother me, and he's the first man I met that it didn't bother either. We had separate bank accounts up until fairly recently but we closed them and now we have a joint account and a joint card. That's been tricky. That's been where the problems arise around money, because if I go to the ATM and take out money and put it in the book, what he does is ask, 'For what?' And I'm like, 'Well, I don't mind telling you but I do mind you asking. I don't ask you if you go to the ATM, I don't even look. I have no idea.' It's a gender issue, I think, but my not working has a lot to do with it."

In Donna's situation there is a dramatic economic imbalance between husband and wife. When I saw her, Donna sat nursing her amiable baby in an apartment high above the city. Modern paintings hang on the dark wood paneling amid an eclectic mix of furnishings, some highly styled modern pieces, some old wood, some overstuffed upholstery. Married about a year, Donna is thirty-six; her husband is in his fifties and has grown children from his first marriage. Donna says she is happy and that the marriage and the baby have given her husband a new lease on life. But the financial aspects of the relationship kept coming up during the interview: "Most girls think that marrying money is easy but in this era you confront, first of all, a prenuptial agreement. It's funny, my husband has sons from his first marriage, and he says, 'The boys should get briefed on what a prenuptial agreement is.' Well, I think women in college should learn what a prenuptial agreement is."

As she was explaining the details of her financial contract, Donna stopped, gestured around the room, and said: "Like, this beautiful place is his according to the agreement. And I emotionally had to say, Okay, do I not clean it because this is his place? What I contribute to the marriage is priceless. We have this beautiful child, and my husband and I are very good friends. I give him confidence, I give him advice. If he's down, he'll call me and he'll talk to me about his problems about work or his family problems. So I'm earning my keep. Then, too, my mom is a successful businesswoman, and what I learned from her, as a woman, is the fact that I can go out there and earn money and be an equal partner in a marriage if I want to. I don't feel inferior because I'm a female. I can take care of myself."

Money can affect the marital balance in subtle ways: Gloria is the director of a highly respected program for children and is well-known in the Mexican-American community. We met in her office where, once in a while, a parent would come to the door. The grace and authority with which she dealt with problems was striking, as was the silvery laugh that ricocheted around the large room when a toddler in her father's arms leaned over to whisper something in Gloria's ear.

Gloria says her husband is proud of her and, as we saw in the previous chapter, he's been encouraging her to try for her soon-to-retire boss's job. "That's not the whole story," she says. "He also feels that his job with the telephone company is more important than mine because he makes more money and I work with kids. He'll understand when I come home and I'm tired and I say I've had a really hard day. Yeah, okay. But because he makes more money, his being tired must be harder. In that part, the sexist thing is there, I don't think it will change. We have our arguments sometimes. The answer is, this field, because it's mostly women, should have better pay. The way to appease myself is I teach the little girls here that they can be anything. When you grow up, you could be whatever. I think our girls are real strong because of that."

Alice's husband made a good living but, she thinks, overextended himself financially as a device to control his wife and children. His tyranny over them was abetted by his unilateral decision to buy the expensive home he "gave" them. As a result, when someone needed money for what he considered a luxury, he could say they couldn't afford it.

Alice and I sat drinking Cokes on the ground level of that elaborate house, the Fourth of July decorations of a few days earlier still festooned around us. It was an incongruous setting in which to speak of matters I suspect had not been given voice before: "I don't think all marriages are made in heaven, and I think that divorce is certainly preferable in many instances to remaining in a bad marriage. We've brought it up, I've thought about it, but in this state, in this county, a Protestant would never have gotten custody of Catholic children. I would have lost them. And if I had divorced my husband I would have fared very poorly. I would never have been able to support my children or myself on what I could make. And then I think probably when things were not good, I took some comfort in material things. I bought a lot of antique silver and other good things. They were a trap but they don't yell, and they give you a momentary or transitory feeling of pleasure."

The Money-Macho Link

....
The women and/or their husbands tend to link the man's ability to earn a living with his masculinity.
....

We heard Ginger, in the chapter on sexuality, getting ready to leave her high-salaried job in an effort to improve the couple's intimate relationship. Of her husband's earning power, she says: "There are days my husband's very stressed-out, saying, 'I've got to get out, I need to get out.' And I say, 'Fine. You want to give up on this place, I'm outta here. You want to go live in a little town, I'm outta here, let's go. I'm ready for a new adventure, and I'm totally happy to have you blow it off.' Now, how that would affect my view of him as a man is on a different level. As my friend and teammate, I'd certainly accommodate him. But to be really honest, I would probably feel he can't handle it. I think I would be responding on two levels, one is to accommodate him as my buddy, and the other one, as a man, I might feel he wasn't quite adequate, because he couldn't earn a good living."

A few of the young women worry about what will happen to their marriages if their husbands never get their financial act together. Anne, a successful investment adviser, is twenty-nine: "I don't think my husband will ever earn more than I do. I can support myself in what I want to do and what we want to do together. I don't need him financially and I don't even need to have my dream right now, but I don't know how he'll do in the long run. Even now, he gets cranky when he's not feeling good about himself. And it always comes back to his job, to money. It's about him needing to feel like he's producing in that area of life like other men do."

Carol puts the dilemma in feminist terms: "A few years ago, when I was questioning the marriage, I had to deal with what his earning potential was and I'm still dealing with it. It's hard to talk about because I have so many conflicting emotions. As a feminist, I feel like he doesn't owe me anything, he's doing what he wants to—although he's not exactly happy doing it, that's part of the problem. But the thing is, he's never really gotten off the dime. At times I throw a lot of energy into pushing him, and then I feel, Oh, God, that's just such an old-fashioned, crazy way. If you want more, if you need more, then go out and make it happen. Just leave this guy alone."

Linda says: "One of the reasons I married my husband was that I thought he'd be a good provider. His father and mine both made a good living but he told me the other day that the maximum he can expect to make on his job is about forty thousand a year. With two kids we just barely make it through the month, and it's a big disappointment. He feels he's a loser, it weighs on him heavily. But when I ask myself whether his wanting more will motivate him to do more for himself in his career, I have to say no. He may not be capable of pulling himself out. We keep going downhill. Yesterday I was in church and my hose were ripped and I had to use nail polish to keep it from running more. The pants I'm wearing have holes in them so while I'm talking to you, I try to remember to keep my legs crossed."

ECONOMIC CONTROL

It takes some digging to figure out who has financial control in a marriage. The women begin by saying things like "I do the checks." Often, though not always, managing the checkbook and paying the bills has little to do with control. More important are questions like: Who handles investments? Who decides when to get a new car and what model to buy? If one spouse needs something expensive—skis, a new winter coat—does the couple discuss it? Who makes the final decision? Who's considered more extravagant, and how does the closer-fisted spouse react? Who is the family bookkeeper, who the comptroller?

> More than half the husbands control family finances. About a third of the wives do. The remaining couples seem to have fairly equal financial power.

The management of family money is tied to income—but also to gender. When husbands earn more, twice as many of them control finances as do their wives; there is little equally shared control. When the wife earns more, the women control finances only somewhat more often than the men, and in about a third of these marriages couples have equal control. Where earnings are about equal, half the couples share control over family money, but more men than women still manage the finances.

Generation may also matter: Among the women in their twenties, half the couples have equal control and the women earn very close to what their husbands do. However, it remains to be seen what will happen as careers develop and children come.

> With only a few exceptions, the women who do not have income of their own or who earn a great deal less than their husbands feel powerless. They say they have little or no control in matters of money or in other significant decisions.

Rachel describes such a situation: "My husband has always made a great deal more than I made and he had an attitude which I guess he got from his father. My parents' household certainly didn't run this way. He made the money and he gave me a household allowance. And while I knew what he was making every year from the tax forms, as far as how much we had, I never knew. The only way I found out anything at all is from filling out a college financial aid form. And as far as what it costs to run this house, I don't know. I asked to pay the bills, I told him to give me the right amount of money and let me take care of it because he's careless and procrastinates about things that need getting done. But he wouldn't let me do it, as a matter of control. For a long time, he used that. I didn't have any money and therefore I didn't have any power even though he never came out and said, 'It's my money and we're going to do it this way.'

"I had some money I had saved. But when the children were small and I wasn't working at all and didn't have any income I could count on, I was reluctant to spend my own money because I didn't know how I would replace it. While I had that little cushion there, if things got too bad, I at least had that leaving-money, enough so that you could think you could leave.

"He still makes decisions on his own, whether we paint the house or not, for example, or buy a car. But we're fixing to have a real role reversal. One reason I've been far happier recently is that since I've been working I have not felt that tight for money. It isn't that he was stingy but that he had all the money and all the power. Once I started work, I wasn't so afraid to make him mad either, as I used to be. And now I will inherit money from my daddy and that's going to change things, not make me wealthy, but he left a right sizable estate of a small nature. It will certainly make a difference in my life-style. I'm going to go ahead and do the stuff on the house that's needed doing a long time. I won't be dependent on my husband, though it won't be enough that I wouldn't have to work if I were ever on my own."

Jeannette's girlhood expectations were unlike the view she now has of the money-power balance: "Initially I resented having to contribute financially. I said, 'You know, I'm not from the background where the wife had to kick in, because most of the wives that I knew from my background, my mother's friends, weren't working. Any money my mother made, she kept for herself. So this 'Where's your down payment for the house? Where's your part for the vacation? Can you buy your own ticket?' I didn't like it but I didn't have a choice. I mean, if you're going to have a partnership and call the shots . . . Like when I moved in with him I'd put my pictures up, and I'd come downstairs the next day and he had taken them down and put them someplace. I moved his stuff around, and he'd put it back and we would do this silently back and forth. But when you've put up 45 percent of the down payment, like I have on our house, you can say, 'Well, this is my 45 percent. I want this room to decorate the way I want to, and to keep it the way I want to.'"

A few older women came to a new understanding of their marriages when they began to earn their own money. Flora is a delicately made woman who dresses with a conservative neatness enlivened by the sense of color that also informs her work as a textile designer. She and her husband were born in Europe and from the sound of it, he was very much the traditional patriarch: "When I first began to sell my designs and we could see that I was going to be earning real money, my husband said, 'I hope this isn't going to change our relationship. It's very important to me and I wouldn't want anything to spoil it.' I assured him that it wouldn't change but of course it did. It was subtle but it was real. My husband was always generous, anything I wanted I could have. There was never any question about what I did with money. But it was his to begin with. He earned it. Now it was different, it was *my* money, money I was getting for my own work. There was a shift in the way we related to each other. We didn't really talk about power, but the power shifted."

Power also shifts when women who have been earning money leave their jobs to stay home, at least temporarily, when a child is born. We've heard Linda say that her husband's earning prospects are limited. She herself has made little money since her two small children were born: "Before I stopped working we both used to take care of the checkbook and for the monthly bills, I was the check writer. He's decided he's going to do that from now on because I've made mistakes. He feels he'll be able to have better control and that one hand in the pudding is best, that he should be the one writing checks because two people shouldn't handle one checkbook. It's also his opinion about me intellectually. He's felt I was stupid in terms of numbers, and I'm not. I couldn't have gotten this far if I had been, I have a master's degree, after all. So I made a subtraction error, so what? I've worked as a financial secretary, and my husband wouldn't even trust me with the checkbook! One of my angers is that he jokingly says, 'I make the money, I bring home a paycheck.'"

Using money management to disparage the other partner came up a few times. Kay remembers: "We'd had a fairly large wedding, but we didn't get any linens and so we went to a store that was having a January white sale. I looked around and said to the saleswoman, 'I'll take two of those, and two of those, and two of those,' pointing to sheets and pillowcases and other things we needed. The saleswoman added it all up, and it came to fifty-four dollars or something like that. My ex-husband said to me, in front of her, in front of the saleswoman, 'All right, you don't have enough money. You're going to have to put some back.' I was humiliated but I didn't say, 'Well, you horse's behind, this stuff is half for you.' On the way home he told me I had spent the food money for the whole week on those things. He wanted to let me know who was in charge from the very beginning, and that's how he did it."

Another one-sentence quote from Kay's former husband reinforces the effect. Because she had four children and a lot of company, Kay says she was continually in the kitchen: "Sometimes I would ask my husband about a dishwasher, I really needed one. But every time I brought it up, time and time again, he would answer, 'Well, I always thought I married one.'"

These last examples make financial power in marriage seem more one-sided than it is. Some women do control the family money for various reasons. Martha has an ironic insight into why things work that way in her marriage: "Until recently, when I got him to participate more, my husband would come home, throw his paycheck on the mantel, and I did everything. I budgeted, I managed, I invested, I did the income tax, I talked to the accountants. I don't think he even knew what bank the vault was in. I think it's that he wants to be free to be an intellectual, a great lawyer, an academic. He just doesn't need the power of the money and he doesn't want to be bothered."

A surprising number of the women allow their husbands to handle family money because they themselves "hate that stuff" or are "not good at it" or "don't want to be bothered." Hope, by her own account, colludes in her husband's economic control: "My husband takes care of the checkbook. I guess I've gotten used to it but it has been a huge bone of contention. One of our biggest fights when we first got married was over that, because I said when I divorced my first husband that I was never going to turn my paycheck over to a man again. But when we moved to where his job was, I had no money, I'd had to leave my own job to go with him—and I was pregnant. It was devastating, absolutely devastating. And I actually didn't make enough money again to make a difference or to get back in an equal situation until we moved down here. But the pattern was already in place. My husband makes the financial decisions. He says he wants me to be more involved than I am but I find it very difficult because the way he's set it up is very different from the way I'd do it. I probably don't participate as much as I could because I hate dealing with finances and I'm not good at it. But I should work at it, it's really to my detriment that I don't."

A recently married woman in her twenties says: "I started making a lot of money when I became a lawyer and I was somewhat irresponsible with it, maybe because I never had it before. When I got it, it was: Woooh! Let's get stuff. So now, when we're married and my husband wants to handle the money, I'm happy to let him do it. His family had money, and he knows more about it. I could run my own money if I had to—I've done it. But he likes to take care of it and I don't care."

MONEY ISN'T EVERYTHING, IS IT?

> Though relationships are severely stressed by unrealized financial expectations or because of real economic problems, not one of the women divorced because of issues of money.

Good marriages seem to survive financial problems and even in the troubled marriages, money was not the straw that broke the camel's back. That is partly because relationships are so complex, partly because there are constant negotiations, largely nonverbal, around this subject. Here's an example: When Hilda married forty-five years ago, she wanted to work and understood that her husband was not interested in making money. Hilda carries with her, out of the tragedy of her childhood—a mother's death, a father's abuse—certain vulnerabilities from which her husband's attentive cosseting protects her. But they live on a two-way street: "There was a time, in my forties, when I got resentful of having to work so hard. I felt, I'm tired, I need to take a year off, I need to stop. I'm not a machine. My husband said, 'You do it, we'll live on less.' I didn't want to live on less. We had the kids, they've got music lessons, orthodontia, this and that, we can't live on less. He said, 'I'm happy in my work, you need time, you take time. It's all right, when we're broke they'll go to community college.' I didn't want them to go to community college. He didn't say what I was hoping, he didn't say that he'd go out and get a job. But now I don't resent it. I understand that I'm less independent about a lot of things. One example is I'm weak on the car. I could figure things out but I'm not that confident a driver, I'm a little afraid. My husband feeds into that—and I'm glad he does. He's not doing what men do economically but he takes care of me in many ways where I'm not strong, so it's convenient for both of us. I think it's a tradeoff. Probably if I had a husband who was killing himself making a lot of money, working hard, I would be ashamed to ask him, 'Would you pick me up?'"

One of the crucial factors in the successful accommodation of this marriage is that Hilda's husband is happy in his work. Obviously he does not need a flow of income to fuel his self-esteem. He gets that from his work, even though it hardly pays in conventional terms. In truth he disdains the admixture of money and art.

I heard a variation on this theme from a foundation administrator in Boston: "I was an idealist when we married in the Fifties, and I honestly don't think I cared much about money. I still don't. But my husband became so bitter over the years about never figuring out what he wanted to be when he grew up and earning so little. He walked around with his fists clenched, and I was the nearest target. We lived okay, I made a decent salary, that wasn't it. His self-respect was the problem for both of us. I wanted a husband who was proud of himself. I wouldn't have cared if he was an artist whose work didn't sell. I would have loved that."

Have things changed for the younger women? Somewhat, but there still are familiar resonances. Stella, thirty-six, lives in Baltimore, where she goes to work every day while her husband is at home with the children: "We only have one income and it's a woman's income, not a man's. There are a lot of things we can't buy. We can't compete with the kids who bring in to school the Ninja Turtles. We don't have money for music lessons, for ballet lessons, or gym. I've had days when it was lentil soup again for dinner and I've said, 'Look, you're not supporting me in the manner to which I was accustomed.' I thought before I married him that he would be a good provider. He was working, and I thought the money would go on. Now I don't think he'll ever make money. Our friends draw me aside and tell me to encourage him to get outside work. They've made him feel that he's not doing what he should in male terms. He struggles with his stature as a male and being able to provide in a traditional way and that has bad effects on our marriage."

This takes us back to where we began this chapter, to what the women expected before marriage. They did not want to marry men who, because they could not earn a living, would not be respected and, worse, would have no self-respect. Whatever the fairness of such a judgment, from what the women say—except in rare instances where there are acceptable tradeoffs—husbands in this predicament do turn out to be hard to live with. The marriage may be undermined by questions of esteem from both sides of the aisle. We still, as the Chinese say, "give face" to men who make a lot of money and to women who are candidates for the Mom of the Year award. They're blurring a little, but the gender lines drawn generations ago to define family responsibilities are still clearly discernible. And, from what they say, I'm not sure that many of the women I talked to would want it otherwise.

9

THE MARRIAGE CONTRACT

f the conditions of married life were spelled out and written down like those of an employment contract, you could be confident that you were at least arranging for the marriage you expect. And you could pull out the agreement from time to time to check whether the parties were living up to the bargain.

The promises we make at our wedding don't cover the specifics of daily life but, in reality, married people operate as if a contract is in place. From the beginning, they assume that both parties share the same expectations and have signed up for the same kind of marriage. That is the principle on which the women I talked to proceeded; their husbands must have felt the same way. People wouldn't marry if they didn't think they knew what they were getting into.

CONTRACT TERMS

Because the contract was unspoken, it was as if the couple was signing a binding agreement, blindfolded. Few of the women verbalized either to themselves or to their future husbands what they thought they were agreeing to.

Since the terms were invisible, they may have been radically different for each signatory. The parties may turn out to have contracted for lives that could not mesh. We have heard Miriam say that she thought marriage meant a nice home and salmon patties. She went on to acknowledge: "Later I realized my husband was looking for a trophy, a pretty girl who'd never put on weight and never get her period."

....

Whatever the original deal, as times and conditions change, as people mature, careers develop, children are born, the contract terms may no longer serve.

....

The marriage contract is, in one respect, like the Constitution: Agreed to when the country was founded, its provisions are relied on to govern the way things work long after the signing. The marriage contract also is meant to serve "till death do us part," but it lacks language to cover new conditions or a Supreme Court to adjudicate relevance or differences in interpretation. Changes can be absorbed only if both husband and wife acknowledge a new situation and stretch to accommodate it. It is when there is a lag or disagreement in recognizing and integrating the changes that trouble looms—that people say in various ways, "This isn't what I anticipated. You are no longer the person I agreed to marry. You're not honoring the deal I thought we made."

When Cornelia married forty years ago, she and her husband embarked on a traditional marriage. As it turned out, he did not support the family, her job took off. But she thinks something else caused her divorce: "The real thing is that I was a different person than the one he married. My job, and feminist ideas, and just being out in the world, all that stuff was changing me. And he didn't like the new woman in the house. He thought I talked too much or, I don't know, maybe that I took my work too seriously. I couldn't have told you back then why I was so desperate to get out but now I see I would have spent my whole life apologizing for the things I like most about myself."

Natalie's contract did not quite fit from the beginning, and it never changed: "I wanted a double-ring wedding ceremony and my husband's response was, his father doesn't wear a wedding ring and he's not going to wear one. Why did I have to? Because it's traditional that women wear wedding rings and men don't. After that I recognized without necessarily putting it in words, that we'd be okay as long as he would be the dominant person and have the dominant career. That also meant he'd support us and I'd do the work at home. Our marriage started at Point A with certain definitions, and we just kept living it by those old definitions. Later, when I was getting involved with the feminist movement and starting my career, my husband understood indirectly. But it didn't change his behavior because we were still locked in the old patterns and we weren't really talking about changing our marriage. I was going out and getting psychiatric help, trying to get myself fixed, which meant get myself back to living under the old contract, where my husband's needs and my husband's career were what drove the marriage."

Natalie divorced years ago. Martha, still married, says: "When I was first married I had strong beliefs in a role-differentiated life; the woman was almost there to serve the man, to be the homemaker and take care of things. I've changed those beliefs and I've changed my ideas of how I would negotiate a marriage if I were doing it again or if I were a young girl today. But I really believe that you get married with a certain contract. Maybe you can modify it but I can't say to a man who was born fifty-five years ago, Now become like somebody who's twenty-five. It would be unrealistic to think that all of a sudden he's going to do half the grocery shopping."

Making Changes

In chapter 8 Lorraine described her shock when she realized that the life in the home she had contracted for was coming to an end: She was going to have to help support the family. But then she saw her marriage change because her teacher-husband, in charge of children and house the first summer she went out to work, gained a new understanding of the hard job she had. From then on, she reports, they were equal partners in both the work and home compartments of their lives, and their marriage flourished.

Stella discussed her ideals and goals with her husband before they married but: "What I've discovered that was different from my expectation is that I thought you got married and that was the end of the story, like Cinderella. But marriage is basically a mandate to change; you sign a contract saying that I will now change forever, from now on I will be continually in the process of changing in order to make it possible to live with this other person."

Ginger is a feminist whose original contract was for an egalitarian marriage, shared moneymaking, shared home-duty. Things have changed for a couple of reasons: "Because I want it done my way, because I want the linen closet just so, the fact is, it is a very unequal distribution at home. I do most of it. I'm definitely like all those statistics: I have two jobs."

On the other hand Ginger is about to turn the financial clause of her marriage contract upside down: "I'm in the midst of a huge change in my life, leaving my job, but my greatest fear is that I'm going to have to ask for money. I always have felt so unbelievably self-reliant. I'm actually trusting, for the first time, that he won't pull a power thing. It's really hard for me."

Keeping the Bargain

We've been looking at changing the original contract. Another dilemma faces the signatories:

The parties may not live up to the obligations they committed to.

Despite any implied agreements, the husband may not support the family, the wife may prefer working outside the home to cooking dinner. Or a wife whose income the couple had factored into their original planning may decide to stay home with a child.

Infidelity presented the most dramatic breach. Not one woman's contract carried the stipulation that either partner would sleep with other people. Nobody agreed to an open marriage with affairs allowed. Fidelity was the bargain. In reality (and for a variety of reasons including that the women may not know the reality) it's hard to know exactly how things worked out.

A few women say they had affairs while they were married but that the marriage was already on the rocks; all but one of them divorced, but they say the infidelity was a symptom, not the cause. However, the respondents' voices were tragic when they described their first awareness that their husbands had been with other women. A forty-two-year-old Californian, who, after divorce, thought she'd found her "other half," said: "Our relationship was just so perfect, almost to the point of unbelief. He was the one that pointed out that we were like soul mates. We'd gone away on a romantic weekend, had a great time. He's constantly pouring out his love for me. When we came home that evening we had a strange knock on the door, and he got a little weird. He ended up telling me that he slept with the girl next door. I was devastated. I couldn't believe this was happening. But before we got married, I knew this potential existed because he had told me the situation with his previous wife where he cheated on her all the time. But that's how we make everything okay in our minds. We say that with me it's going to be different. It was the last thing I expected, the worst thing. I couldn't in my wildest dream imagine that I could still love someone after this. In fact, when I was really going through the pain and anger, I didn't want to love him. Now I think it's behind us. He's getting some therapy and he really wants this marriage to work."

Like most women with this experience, a New Englander of fifty-two couldn't believe that this could be happening to her, either the first time or ever again: "I was giving my youngest a bottle when my husband told me that he'd been having affairs with three women, but they were over and that was all behind us. I was absolutely horrified but that wasn't the end of the marriage, because I trusted him. I assumed that this was never going to happen again. It did happen again, once with another close friend, a tennis-playing friend. I was outraged when I found that out. I called her and I said, 'How could you do this to me?' At that point the kids were screaming at the door while I'm making this telephone call. I yell for the summer girl to come up and get them and the woman on the phone says to me, 'God, you still have that girl? Your husband had an affair with her last year, and while we're on the subject, he also had an affair with your college roommate.'"

This woman had married while she was still in college; the roommate was in the wedding party but surely not in the contract.

What Kind of Marriage Do We Believe In?

....

There is one unwritten clause that obviates the need to spell out each contract detail: If the partners share a defined value system, they have a built-in guide with which to approach the challenges of marriage. Some of the strongest relationships included couples with such values.

....

This factor has little to do with the rhetoric of "family values." In this group of women, there are atheists, traditional Asians, humanists, ardent feminists, recovering alcoholics, and observant members of various religions. Whatever their belief, both parties have articulated a commitment to live according to certain principles. The women in such marriages say things like "We don't believe in that"; or "Our faith helped us"; or "Socialists know about each according to need"; or "Our children don't get paid for doing chores"; or "My kids have to understand they're part of a larger family"; or "We went to AA together, we both know what we want now."

Obviously there are failed relationships among political activists, devout Catholics, and vegetarians. But in marriages in which the women and their husbands hold their daily lives up to the same measure, there is less likely to be long-term trouble. Jane and her husband are Japanese-American: "What this marriage is about is that we are both working together to the benefit of each other, but more to the benefit of the children. We set goals together when we were young and we made plans to fulfill them, that's what we worked towards. It's not just the physical part here in this house, but also ideologically, that this is what family is about. And it fits into the larger family, of the grandparents and the other relatives. The children have been told, even as they're dating, if there's a family event, you need to be courteous and show up, and then if you're going out on a date, that's fine. Or you need to call and tell them why you're not attending."

Maria, twenty-six, had a serious drinking problem. Cecile, thirty-two, used drugs. They both married men with similar substance abuse problems; all of them have been substance-free for some time. Both women seem incredulous at the happiness in their marriages, grateful for their husband's emotional support, especially gentle in speaking about the way they get on. Maria said: "I drank a lot before marriage, I have the gene. And now that I was married I had someone who drank with me, both of us had a problem, so there was no risk of anyone ever scolding you. When I stopped drinking the thought in my mind was, I can't believe I have this wonderful man and this life that's better than I ever imagined, and I'm drinking. Why am I doing this? We stopped at the same time through AA and that intensified our commitment to each other because we did it together. We've both changed a lot because of what we went through. We didn't face things or discuss things the way we should when we were drinking and now we do."

When I asked Vivian how she was able to maintain a compatible marriage while raising twelve children, she poked her chin in the direction of a crucifix on the wall: "Well, we both had faith, that helped a lot." Vivian had supported her sons' opposition to the Vietnam War. She also had strong ideas about women's rights: "Before the children were born, when I was a P.E. teacher, the male coaches got paid for the extra work and the women didn't. I went to the school board and tried, but they told me the men had families to support and we didn't. I believe in equal pay, and now my daughters do get paid fairly. My mother was an old feminist too. I never made the beds for my brothers, and I never had my daughters wait on the boys. That's the way the marriage and the family worked for me and my husband and the children—with feminist rules."

But values and goals aren't always communal property. We've heard that Anne is working toward the kind of life her parents provided—the waterfront house, the sailing, tennis, and skiing. By making careful plans and investing well, she is on her way: A first house is under construction, her own lucrative career has been launched. Her husband, however, hasn't yet found what he wants to do: "He has this thing. In his family, you have to do something that has meaning. I was not raised like that at all. Even though I feel like what I do has a lot of value— it's an all-woman firm and we provide a great financial service that helps people out—my husband would probably say that in my job, I'm not saving starving children or doing anything that outwardly is advancing this country forward. He's really into environmental stuff and he'll probably do something like that. That's because of his strong feeling of, I have to do good. Making money is just not consistent with that but I really do admire it in him."

If both partners share articulated ethical values, they are more likely to be operating under the same marital contract and to get what they expect from marriage. It's part of a pattern we've been picking up: Many of the happiest women did not start out as dreamy girls; they seem to have understood the connection between goals—which grow out of values—and the choices they made.

The Negotiators

Certain of the women, "the negotiators," did discuss the contract before the wedding and did attempt at least to air the issues.

As we saw earlier, almost everyone decided to marry because she was in love. But the negotiators fell in love, agreed to marry, and then, before the trip down the aisle, began their transactions. In varying detail they discussed children, career, money, and the division of home-front responsibilities. They did not confine themselves to romance or dreams but tended to "get down to brass tacks." It was as if, like their great-grandmothers, they were making arranged marriages but arranging them themselves. This pattern was often related to generation. Half the younger women and only a few of those beyond their mid-forties had such discussions. However, because the decision to marry a particular person was made *before* these conversations took place, they usually had only a limited effect on the actual marriage.

Lucy married as a teenager; nevertheless: "Even being at a very young age, I knew what I wanted. I had a strong feminist attitude and I wasn't going to be in a marriage where I was expected to do all the domestic responsibilities. We really did talk about how roles were not defined by sex. We talked about children, whether or not we wanted to have them, how many we wanted, that kind of thing. When we first got married he was doing domestic stuff right away, we'd agreed on all that beforehand. But in the beginning we had to define those things and figure out how they were going to work."

Some of the younger women lived with their boyfriends before marriage, and though such arrangements are outside the parameters of this book, it doesn't sound as if people discussed the issues of "moving in" as carefully as they did the issues of marrying. A few women broke off relationships with men they'd lived with and, in that sense, did have a trial period in which to test some of the unspoken terms. But many of the conditions of actual married life didn't come up—child care, for example; and money was not really pooled. It wasn't until marriage loomed that much negotiating took place.

GETTING ALONG
Home-Front Duties

The subject's been written about again and again but household chores provide a litmus paper to test how the marital contract plays out in daily life, how the nitty-gritty holds up to what people expected.

To begin with, most of the women say that once there are children, it is the wife who is responsible for the daily management, if not the actual drudgery, of the household. Some couples share the work; very few husbands do more than their wives.

....

Generally speaking, when they married, the younger women expected that they and their husbands would be equally responsible for running the home. They don't always get that in the long run. The older women signed up for the housekeeping, but the arrangement doesn't serve when they work outside the home, as almost all of them eventually do.

....

I heard everywhere the scenario Carol described: "As in most of these modern marriages, I'm in charge, and I sort of dole out the work. I can't stand it but if I don't tell him what to do, he won't do anything. Some things we have totally regimented. For example, every week he does the shopping. He gets my second son ready for school, he makes their lunch. If you looked at it on the surface, you'd maybe say he does as much as he can. It's just that I have to manage it, I have to nag. And I don't like it, I don't know any woman who likes that job. We've had a lot of discussions and sometimes, where I'm on the verge of a breakdown here, then he'll shape up and for a few weeks he'll do stuff without my asking him. He used to tell me it's because we have different standards, that he doesn't care about cleanliness and that stuff, but he knows now I won't put up with that."

> Homework is related to earnings. In families where household chores are equally shared, more than half the wives earn as much or more than their husbands. But whatever their age, whatever each partner's income, as we've seen, there are few husbands who do more work at home than their wives.

Married to the CEO of a large business, Donna has household help but does many of the daily chores herself. Her husband does not help and also expects her to do certain traditional "wifely" tasks: "He's used to having everything done for him, everything's handed to him. Whereas he comes home and maybe something's not done, he gets aggravated and picky. I've told him, 'That's office, this is home. Time out, you know. Things are different here. They're not run on a schedule. You're not paying somebody ten, fifteen bucks an hour to get it done for you.' Sometimes when he's on my case about something, I tell him to call his secretary."

Donna sees a quid pro quo, however: "You know, those are things that aren't that important. If I was involved with somebody who had time to cook and time to be thoughtful but yet he didn't have the power that this man has, would I be happier?

These are the tradeoffs that you have when you get the kind of person you're looking for."

The way Donna interprets the marriage contract is a variation of what Hilda said in the previous chapter—that perhaps if her husband were out working hard to make a lot of money, she wouldn't feel free to ask him to pick her up when she's hesitant to drive.

> Are family chores considered by both men and women beneath the dignity of the rich and powerful? Perhaps that's one of the reasons why men, who generally earn more and have more power, consider the household women's work.

Money isn't the only ball in play. Even couples with the same income get irritable about the house. They're tired, there's too much to do, they don't have enough time for fun— who wouldn't rather have somebody else do the scut work? But there's more likely to be a fair, if crotchety, exchange in situations of economic parity: Rita and her husband are in their thirties. Married for thirteen years, they are still negotiating home-front clauses: "Just two days ago we got into this discussion because my daughter asked, 'How come you do all the cooking, Mom?' I told her to ask her dad about that and he said, 'Because she's better at it than me. It's kind of like a tradition.' I couldn't believe what I was hearing. 'You're saying you're falling into these traditional roles just because? You've totally shocked me.' And then he thought he had me by asking, 'So who does the oil change?' And I said, 'Well, you do because I don't like getting messy. I don't really want to change the oil, but I'm going to learn!' And I really am. Forget this tradition stuff. You only change the oil once in a while. You eat dinner every day!"

In one family husband and wife both have excellent incomes but home-front duties remain a focus of the daily give-and-take: "We don't make supper that much anymore. With a baby, you sort of walk around with, I don't know, oranges on a paper towel. He used to cook all the time, and sometimes I'd try to get him to do the dishes because I hate to. We've always had somebody come in once a week and somebody who did all the laundry. He takes the dry cleaning, I order the food. But we both always feel like we're doing more than the other one. We both feel equally put-upon—which we both vehemently deny. So then you have the litany of: 'I always take care of the baby's doctor.' And he says, 'I'm always the one who drives.' We do it and then that's over. It's pretty even, to tell the truth."

The way respondents talk about household work is very like the talk you hear in offices: Who's doing more work? Who's got more control? Who's getting acknowledgment? Money? On the job we worry about whether things are fair, whether we have our due share of power, whether the job we've got measures up to what we signed on for. That's basically what the women are working out. Am I doing—and receiving—my fair share? Is this what I had in mind?

QUARRELING

When the answers to these and other contentious questions are negative, when couples disagree, they confront each other in ways that grow out of their earliest expectations, family patterns, and the emotional work they later do. There has been a great deal said about the value of communication in relationships. I found that the talkers are happier than those who don't discuss problems. The only successful marriages of nontalkers occur among women in their sixties who never expected emotional openness and have made accommodations. And, as we'll see, even among these women, when talking stops, the results can be disastrous.

When there are disagreements some couples rely on "clearing the air" with a directness that seems to affirm the strength of the relationship. Helen describes such a pattern: "From the beginning it was a sort of a met-my-match feeling—if I push will you push back? Now that we're married, sometimes I think we have only one fight. I could practically tape it by now: We're so tired, we don't have sex enough; we don't have a plan for getting out of the city; we don't spend enough time together. I find that oddly reassuring and I chalk it up to being two different people. There are going to be these places that we're different, and at some point there's going to be conflict and it's going to explode once in a while. But every time we repair paths, it gives me new confidence that actually the marriage is as strong as I think it is."

Daisy, twenty-seven, has a career involving employee relations, and she takes her professional methods home with her: "If you're disagreeing about something, I don't think it's enough just to say you're sorry. You have to understand what you're each sorry for, because it could be two totally different things and you'll never really know what's wrong. I see that in my workshops. So I'm always saying, 'What are you sorry about?' or else I'm wanting to tell him why I'm sorry. It used to drive my husband crazy but now sometimes he'll even call me on it. The other thing is that my husband doesn't like his job and it has an influence on how he is at home. When he comes home like that I will be as empathetic as I can, but he needs to know that it's not my fault and that he's talking to me, not at me. I make that clear."

Ginger wants professional backup: "I feel I need to have a shrink connection so that my husband doesn't mess with my mind. I have an arbiter all set up, should the need arise, where we can go. We have emotional power struggles, not nasty ones, but sometimes we've gone over to the point of making me feel vulnerable. The shrink is my safety valve."

Linda describes a situation in which no mechanism has been developed to settle disagreements. In fact, her husband apparently never expected quarrels between them: "My husband has told me he's disappointed in the marriage because there's a lot of bickering he didn't anticipate. He doesn't like the fact that we disagree on so many things. Because of our family backgrounds I scream and my husband closes up. We have these fights and he's controlling himself and I'm pushing him to uncontrol himself because it makes me angrier when he doesn't. It irritates the hell out of me, just like it irritates him that I'm so bossy and tear him down so much. Why am I doing that?"

The marriage contract is betrayed most disastrously when physical abuse is used to deal with disputes. This account is from a woman of fifty-four whose husband left her when she sought help from a center for abused women: "He started getting physically abusive the first week we were married, hitting me. When I talked to my mother, she told me to be patient, he'll change. I confided in his business partner who said he'll mellow. That was what they told women in those days, Just be sweet. And he abused me sexually, always. He was this authority figure so I was confused all the time—what's wrong with me that I can't do better? He abused me in front of the children and he thought that was great, that was power. If I tried to discuss it with him, he'd throw me across the room, or not give me money, or leave."

Sometimes, even without so extreme a problem, when circumstances or people change, old modes of relating no longer serve. A few women in their late fifties and early sixties, some divorced, some still married to their first husbands, used almost the same language this respondent did: "I had a sense in my first marriage that I had to be a good girl. That was the deal we made. Later, when I just couldn't stand being a good girl anymore, of course the marriage broke up."

It is from Lisbeth that we hear the heartbreak of a complete shutdown of communication. With blonde hair, regular features, and skin that has been weathered by a lifetime of skiing and tennis, Lisbeth also has an athlete's careless, proud bearing. The day I spent with her, she wore tapered black pants, a black wool-and-satin vest, a well-cut white cotton blouse. It was a very different style from the deliberately down-played look of the women in the Western community in which she lives. But it is Lisbeth's cheerful, slightly mocking self-presentation that is most striking. It's as if she's amazed but not unhappy to find herself where she is at this late date, living alone in an apartment, in a new town: "Many times during the years we were married, he'd just blow up at something. Then he wouldn't speak to me for three or four weeks. Once he didn't speak to me for a year. Meals were silent. I'd put the food on the table and go eat in the kitchen. That was his biggest punishment, not to speak to me. Towards the end, when things were really deteriorating, he was silent more and more often. Towards the end the silence was like a scream in my house.

"If I ever confronted him, he'd say, 'Hey, you don't like it, get going. I got along just fine before I met you. I'm sure I'll get along.' And the hatred? Sometimes it would just come out of every pore. He would shout and bang things around, slam drawers and doors. I never thought he was going to hit me but it was frightening because it's such a change in a person. Their eyes change, their nostrils flare . . . To this day, this man doesn't have a clue of how I felt or what he did. He thinks I left because I got liberated. He thinks I'm not the person he married. How come he doesn't know? I can't understand it. I would say to him, 'Nobody can live in this silence and with the way you treat me.' He'd answer, 'I've treated you perfectly fine. You've always had plenty of money. You've always had your own car.' There have been times I've been on my knees weeping, 'Please tell me what I've done wrong, please tell me why you're acting this way. How can I make you love me more? What can I do to make you happy?' And he wouldn't answer me. He'd turn his back on me and ignore me. I'm so ashamed of that. I am. I am. The best thing is that I left."

THE BALANCE OF POWER

Very often the issues couples face have to do with power. Sometimes the invisible contract concedes control from the beginning as Daisy describes: "I just think that my personality is stronger than his. We've talked about that, we both know it. It's really important to me to not ever take advantage, partly because I know it."

The question has also always been clear for Martha: "My husband is definitely much more dominating. He's somebody who is very articulate and very intellectual, and whatever he's doing at the moment, he'll master the subject, he'll read it, he'll remember the whole thing, he'll recite it to you. I tend to get quiet in a social setting, and if he's in an area, I scout someplace else. Not that he would be threatened by my coming—it's my sense of inadequacy, that I couldn't measure up. He's much smarter than I am. I think I'm smart but he's enormously smart."

In other marriages there is no power clause and the couple jockeys for position, as Helen describes: "We're both constantly struggling to have more power. We have sort of bowling ball personalities. Even though he's quieter than I am, it's always sort of back and forth. But I also think that's half the interest. I was attracted to him for the same reason. Sometimes it's acrimonious: You hurt my feelings, you picked on me. I do feel bossed around sometimes and I'm sure he does too. You always take it seriously but because we've been through it so many times, you just let it go. We both know we're doing that and it's a sort of peacemaking."

And sometimes things are not what they seem. Sue Ellen appears to hold the power in her marriage. She handles the money, makes family decisions, goes her own way most of the time. But, miserable with her life, Sue Ellen seems pinned in place: "A few years ago I filed for divorce. He made it very difficult, by simply, number one, refusing to discuss it, which is the bottom line that he does with everything, refuse to talk about it, always say, 'I want to make it work.' And then he had this wonderful passive-aggressive tactic that stymied everything. He refused to even open the letters from my attorney. That went on for a protracted period of time and by that point—well, I got very sick and it was like, Why even bother? Where do I find the strength and the money to keep battling?"

TOGETHER VS. INDEPENDENT

Whatever their early expectations, how much time do married people actually spend together, how much time on their separate interests? When you contract to get married, just how much togetherness are you agreeing to?

We heard Lisbeth speak of the long silences in her marriage. Her life with her husband eventually had few points of contact: "The community got used to the fact that he didn't ever do anything socially. I always went to things alone, the movies or a concert. I had good tennis friends, swimming buddies, and my ski friends. But whenever they had a dinner potluck or something social, well, I didn't go to those. I come from a very sociable family but he didn't want people to come to our house so I'd entertain very little. The best way to explain is to tell you my first Christmas with him. I was twenty-one, and I'd always had a big Christmasy, Christmasy thing. So I prepared the Danish food and all that stuff and after I came back from church at midnight, I said, 'Let's open some presents.' And he said, 'Hell no, I never open my presents until Christmas morning. You can open yours if you want, I'm going to bed.' And from then on that was our routine, he went to bed on Christmas Eve. That was the first slap in the face."

Because Rachel's parents shared so many activities, she expected the same degree of togetherness in her own marriage. The issue has never been resolved: "I think we're going to have some hard times because, with the children going off to college, I'm going to have more free time and start resenting it if my husband's at the golf course or his mother's all the time. It used to make me mad when the children were small and he'd go over to his parents' every afternoon to have his drink. We haven't done much together at all in recent times. We used to play tennis but we don't anymore. I've tried to like some of the sports he watches but baseball on television bores me to distraction. In my family we played sports, we didn't watch them. I hope we can figure out a way to find more companionship.

"When I got to be around forty, I sort of had a reversion to being more like the self that I like, the real me. I think it was a letting go of expectation about marriage, about what it was going to be. I decided that I was going to stop trying so hard. It hurt my feelings that he didn't want to do things with me, but if I wanted to go to a dance, for example, and he didn't, I was going to go. I wasn't going to worry about it. And if people asked me where he was, I'd just say, 'He didn't want to come.' But I don't want my marriage to get like others I see, the husband gone quite a bit on his work and the wife going to Europe with her friends. People like that lead very separate lives. That's not what I had in mind when I married."

In Anne's case it is her husband who complains about her not being available: "I have long hours and the other night my husband said, 'I'm home three hours every night before you get home.' Because he's moved around, he doesn't really have friends here like I do. He wants to go out and ride his bike down steep hills, and he wants to go kayaking in Alaska. In many ways he's always relied on me to be his fun. But now I have a lot of things going on that don't necessarily involve him—work, and business travel, maybe a dinner meeting here and there. I told him I really want him to find somebody who can do things that I can't do with him. I really don't want to go kayaking for a week in Alaska. A day or two maybe, but not a week. I can't take the time."

It used to be mostly men whose work ate into the couple's time together. Now either partner may devote what might have been family time to career. Sometimes, though, the together-separate tension is masking a more complicated agenda. The women seem to be asking questions like: Is he too dependent on me? Do I need from him more than he's giving? They are using talk about business dinners or golf or football on television as a code for discussing dependency and intimacy.

Hope says that sometimes she feels her husband would like to have all her time and attention for himself: "He wants me to be available to him always. He doesn't want me to be busy, he doesn't want me to be sick, he doesn't want me to be emotionally distraught, he doesn't want me to feel oppressed. He relies on my presence and on my strength and if I'm not strong, it's hard for him." Then she stopped and grinned: "That's interesting. I've never verbalized that before and I've been wondering what that business of his needing to be together all the time was about."

And in this passage a woman who wanted more closeness in her marriage describes her now-abandoned dreams: "I've come more to terms with fantasies that I had. I love to travel, and to me having an adventure like that and sharing it with your husband would be wonderful. Well, I had to say, we may go places once in a while, but it may not be wonderful. I changed my expectations so that I didn't have these great disappointments. But with the compromise, I also don't get the great joy.

"The biggest area where it's been a disappointment is that I thought that I would be understood and he would feel understood and cared for in a way that nobody else in the world could, and that would be the most important thing in the marriage, that shared intimacy that would be there between us. That's the dream that's lost. We're no longer aiming for that closeness. I've tried to put an effort into it, but I haven't gotten a response in all these years, and therefore I've said I'm not going to try—because I don't want to get my hopes up and then get crushed."

This woman had begun talking about the love of travel she got from her parents but very soon was talking about intimacy. It was the failure of that quality, not a trip to Timbuktu, that she mourned in her marriage. Her resignation is like Lisbeth giving up on Christmas Eve, or Rachel finding her "real" self by abandoning her expectations for the marriage.

There's also good news. Women point out that the relationship is often enriched by the separate career and social experiences of each spouse. Daisy, young and recently married, says, "I don't think that just because you're married, you have to be joined at the hip. It's important for both of you to have a life outside of the one that you have together. You grow so much when you do that. My husband feels the same way. Sometimes he and his friends take a long weekend and go over to Michigan for a baseball game. They've been doing this for years, way before I met him. There's no reason to stop just because you're married. I think that it helps that we're both sort of independent. It's not that I don't enjoy being with him, I love it, but it's just important to do something with somebody else too."

As another example, both Hilda and her husband work at home. They take an afternoon off together from time to time, and though Hilda used to travel in connection with her work, she now rarely does. Like many older people, this couple spends more time alone together than they ever did, and they seem to have developed a new closeness: "I think now the mutual support is the strongest part. We kind of help each other out. For instance, now that we're getting older, we don't sleep well. I always had a little insomnia, but my husband never did. Now he'll wake up, go to the bathroom, and he can't get back to sleep. And the routine is, I start telling him about Jane Austen, who's one of my idols— ridiculous. Just this morning, at five, he said, 'I've been up since all hours.' And I said, 'Now, in *Mansfield Park,* here's what happens,' and right away, inside of fifteen minutes, he's asleep."

FEMINISM

We've heard some women say that feminism helped shape their expectations and/or the reality of their marriages. Maria says: "I picked one bad boyfriend after another. I was attracted to bad kids, abusive physically and emotionally. I thought, I'm just not good enough for anybody decent to stick around for. I was very scared. Feminism helped me stop what I was doing. When I knew that I wanted to be treated fairly, I felt an obligation to my sex to be strong. I chose to get out of an abusive affair because I wanted to be treated with respect. After that changed, I met my husband."

Women who were feminists to begin with tended to negotiate marriage contracts that were in accord with their beliefs— though only some of them have achieved egalitarian marriages. When they encountered such ideas after they married, the dynamics of the relationship often changed. The original contract terms were perceived as out-of-date. Sometimes the new awareness led to fulfillment for both partners; sometimes the woman's changing consciousness provided her with an explanation of her restlessness or unhappiness (though her husband may have blamed the women's movement).

About half the women say they are feminists, half say they are not. There's not much difference in the success rate of their marriages perhaps because, whatever the semantics, most of them share the same ideas. This phenomenon has been noted elsewhere but it was startling to hear a woman of thirty-six, for example, say defiantly that she was raising her daughter to be "anything she was capable of"—and then add that she was not a feminist. Not one respondent believed in anything less than equal pay for equal work and, in particular, mothers decried the influence of the media on little girls' expectations. Yet they would add, "Well, *that* part's okay. It's the other stuff I don't like." What other stuff? "I think mothers should be allowed to stay home with small children if they want to"; "I hate the idea of abortion"; "I don't believe in bra-burning"; "Black women have always worked"; "I like men." Their words made it sound as if it's a change of rhetoric that's needed for reconciliation, rather than one of philosophy.

....

We make contracts every day: I won't cut in front of you on the supermarket line today, you won't do it to me tomorrow; I'll buy stamps, you'll deliver the mail. We have contracts of longer duration and greater complexity with friends, colleagues, and members of the family. But it is the marriage contract that must last the longest, stretch the farthest, and be reinterpreted with trying frequency. The lives of the respondents bring into sharp relief the importance of being courageous enough to frame an agreement in the first place, of being steadfast enough to live under its governance, and of being flexible enough to pass necessary amendments.

10

OF DREAMS
AND THEMES

W hat is the theme of your marriage?"

"What would the person we began with, you at fifteen, have thought about the way your life has turned out?"

With the answers to these two questions each woman would fashion a neat summary of the reality of her marriage against the background of her girlhood expectations. I had thought that getting at this information would take a fair amount of probing but, by the time we reached this point, we'd been talking for hours. The women were finely tuned to what we were doing and deeply thoughtful about their marriages.

The answers came freely, though sometimes with great sadness. Having to articulate a theme could force a woman to sum up a bad marriage more plainly than she'd ever done before. And the question about expectations can be the most painful of all. Who at fifteen could anticipate the random fall of bad luck on her own life—that, for example, she'd give birth to a blind child? And who, in her youth, would understand the somber regret in the adult phrase, "If only I'd known"?

On the other hand some women felt that though things are different than what they expected, their particular marriage is better than an inexperienced teenager could have imagined. Many of the women who had been thoughtful about marriage choices, the calculators, felt their girlhood expectations had been realized. And occasionally, naming a theme brought a smile of recognition to a woman's face.

Each of the following portraits begins with interview excerpts of the woman's early expectations. That is followed by the theme she herself gave to her marriage, and then by what she believes she would have made of it all when she was a girl. We begin with the oldest women and work toward those in their twenties.

LISBETH

Lisbeth was the only child of outgoing, loving parents. Though she grew up in the 1930s, her vision of adult life was influenced by the women around her who combined marriage and career.

AS A GIRL: "When I was growing up I was really going to be a career woman like my teachers and coaches but I liked boys and I was very social. Anyhow, every girl assumed she would marry. That was sort of in our minds, that you reach this age, twenty-one, and that's the thing to do, get married."

At twenty-one Lisbeth met and married her husband, partly out of idealism—they worked as a medical team during a polio epidemic—partly for the prestige of marrying a doctor. But also important was the sexual attraction that was to continue for many years of their long marriage. Eventually, however, silence became the harsh mode of the couple's communication and Lisbeth began to construct a life of her own outside the relationship.

THE THEME: *"The theme may be that we were married too long*. When our kids were growing up, it was pretty good. He was affectionate, I always slept in his arms. In later years, it was just seething hatred that went on for months and months. We were married over forty years, and what held the marriage together was that I was afraid to leave. And I could always go out and play tennis, come home, have a silent meal, and then go out again to the movies."

Now sixty-seven, Lisbeth left her husband a few years ago and moved to a compact, modern apartment with a view of the mountains and the downtown section of the small city in which she lives. The joy she expresses at her new freedom is tempered by her wistful description of sitting at the window in the evening, watching couples walk to the restaurant downstairs, holding hands, patting each other, laughing.

AT FIFTEEN: "I feel a lot smarter than the girl I was before I got married. When I was that age I never even knew anyone who was divorced so I would have been afraid to think of leaving someone after forty years. I'm rarely lonely now, but talk about lonely! There's nothing more lonely than being in a silent house like I was. A fifteen-year-old couldn't have known something like that."

HILDA

Hilda had a terrible childhood: a sometimes absent, sometimes mentally disturbed mother, a father who sexually abused her after her mother's death. She had to create for herself a picture of what marriage could be like.

AS A GIRL: "I read fairy tales all through childhood. I carried with me the idea of being rescued, rescued, rescued, over and over again. I expected to be free and independent, and yet I wanted to be rescued, and I didn't think about how it would fit together. I wanted a man to be handsome and gallant, to be always there, always steady and understanding. I wanted everything—including my independence."

Hilda married at nineteen. Determined to have a career, in accordance with the marriage contract she and her husband negotiated, Hilda has been the primary breadwinner in her family. The marriage has been nurtured by a pragmatic as well as a more subtle exchange of affection and support.

THE THEME: *"The theme of our marriage is the friendship.* We have fun together and we have a good balance. He's so smart when it comes to what's happening out in the world, he's so smart mechanically. When it comes to literary things and people, I'm smarter, so we kind of share parts of life. Then where he's strong emotionally, I've been a strong provider."

At sixty-five, Hilda and her somewhat older husband seem to have weathered their marital storms—not that their differences have been erased, but that they are less troublesome. She has been financially successful and, in that context, considers her husband's disdain of material things a little mannered. Since the children are grown, Hilda's occasional resentment of the economic burden is no longer relevant; she is free now to appreciate the contribution her husband makes to the marriage.

AT FIFTEEN: "What that young girl would say is,'This wasn't what I planned. I expected to live in a mansion and have a man on horseback riding around. But this is a lot better.' The mutual support is the strongest part. We kind of help each other out."

NATALIE

A Jewish child growing up in Nazi-occupied Holland, Natalie was protected physically and psychologically from the horrors around her by her vigilant parents. She married at nineteen without questioning whether her own needs would be met in the marriage.

AS A GIRL: "When I was a young teenager I had this great romantic notion that the man I would marry, besides being very tall and very good-looking, would be European, that somehow I would go back to my roots and find this great, dramatic, romantic person. Then, when I was a senior in college and was going to all my older girlfriends' showers, I remember just weeping because I wanted to get married, I wanted the safety. I had been in such a cloistered environment with my parents even after the war, that there may have been a part of me that said, 'Hey, if I can get married and avoid that in-between of being on my own, won't that be terrific?' Because I was really scared."

From the time her husband rejected the idea of a double-ring wedding ceremony Natalie believed that, for the marriage to succeed, it was he who would have to be dominant in the relationship. But living with that premise turned out to be very hard, especially because it remained largely undiscussed.

THE THEME: *"The theme of our marriage is that I would say, 'Here's how I feel'; and then my husband would say, 'Here's how it really is.'* We liked and respected each other but that just wasn't enough. I wasn't talking, and he wasn't letting feelings into the relationship. There was no way we could survive."

Now fifty-four and divorced, Natalie has an interesting, entrepreneurial career and fills her free time with her children, friends, sports, and cultural activities.

AT FIFTEEN: "If I could have seen what was going to happen, I'd be sad but if I could know then what I know now, I'd be able to see that I don't really have to go that route, it isn't going to work for me. Why don't I figure something else out? I wouldn't have married at nineteen, I would have waited. But I didn't think I had options when I was fifteen."

NORMA

The daughter of politically radical parents, Norma had dreams that were influenced by the romantic messages of the outside culture and the often conflicting ideology of the community in which she grew up.

AS A GIRL: "When I was a kid, I always thought about having a family. Marriage came along in the bargain—you can't have a family without having a husband. The myth I loved is *The Sound of Music,* the image of falling in love, overcoming circumstances, and then having all those kids! I imagined marrying someone idealistic and together we were going to have six kids and devote our life to making the world a better place for humanity. In our left-wing community, we didn't play games like marriage and dolls. What was stressed was that everyone's the same, sing folk songs together, rather than more traditional feminine things. But I think it went too far to the other extreme. What was lost was the sense of yourself as a sexual being."

Norma married at nineteen but the marriage was always problematic: Her husband was improvident economically and eventually was unfaithful; she did not respond sexually to him and was not willing to work on that aspect of their relationship because, she now believes, she has always been a lesbian.

THE THEME: *"We got married too young.* We were so young we didn't know who we were or what we were doing and we didn't know how to work through any life situation whatsoever, from birth to divorce. But we had these wonderful children and, from my husband, I got a sense of myself as a woman. Despite the unhappiness and the frustrations in my marriage, I'm definitely happy that I didn't have the consciousness to know that I was a lesbian back then."

At fifty-one Norma has been living with her lover in a family situation for many years. But she seems to be contemplating major changes, testing new options.

AT FIFTEEN: "If the girl I was could have seen what my life is like now as a lesbian, maybe she'd like what she saw but I don't think she'd have had the courage to go for it. Or really, she would have been scared even to look at it—because that wasn't what was expected of her. It would have been too painful to see something so enriching that also was outside the realm of what she thought was possible. She would have just ignored it."

JOYCE

Joyce, an only child, was an actress by the time she was four, encouraged and supported by admiring parents. A dreamer, she made up games of marriage and had vivid fantasies straight out of fairy tales.

AS A GIRL: "I had a daydream that my suitors would be lined up in the living room and my father would choose one. I assumed that I would marry a poor actor and make a lovely home for him, and he would become famous and so would I. But somehow I'd be at home. I mean I was going to be an actress but there was also this thing of making for this poor man a lovely home, with flowers everywhere."

Joyce married the first time at twenty-five, the second time at thirty-three, and again at forty-two. Her theme refers to her present marriage.

THE THEME: *"The first theme that came to me is that my husband and I dance very well together. When I hear myself saying that it makes me feel good and also makes me kind of want to cry. We like to hang out together, we have fun doing that, that's happy times for us. This is the first time in a relationship I've felt like we will go on together."*

Now fifty-four, Joyce, from a conservative Catholic family, says affectionately of herself and her husband, "We're sort of old hippies in a way." She seems content with her life, level-headed, but also appreciative of the man she's married to, who is ten years younger than she. According to Joyce, this age difference causes no problems.

AT FIFTEEN: "My present marriage probably would have looked dull and boring to me when I was fifteen because I was really into that whole romantic picture right out of the Fifties, me in the full skirt and the candles and the lace, and whoever he was got rich, and we would be just marvelous to each other. That would have been much more appealing to me. But what did I know? When I was sixteen I thought I had a vocation as a nun. That girl would have been shocked at my life. Dumb! Things have turned out fine."

BARBARA

Barbara grew up in a small southern town, the daughter of a mother who gave her a fair amount of early responsibility and a father who believed "she could do no wrong, or whatever it was could be forgiven." She learned early in her life to make plans, to figure out in advance what she wanted and how to get it.

AS A GIRL: "I think little girls talk about Prince Charming–type husbands but I always knew about statistics, that you do not fight the odds. If statistics say that the chance is a marriage will be improved if your backgrounds are similar, then you'd better not take somebody who is a Zen Buddhist and match him with a Southern Baptist. At the least you've got the same sort of value system underlying what's going on, know that things that are important to you will be important to somebody else. I didn't sit around dreaming much, I worked hard so I could live the way I wanted to live. I wanted a husband who would appreciate all that and would hold up his end. When we started dating, my guard was sort of up, like the guy's got to pass muster before I'm going to turn loose with my heart."

Barbara, as her mother advised her to, married a man who "puts her first." And though her son once characterized her as "queen of the slaves," Barbara seems to make an effort not to lean too hard. For example, though she'd rather say, "I don't do kitchens," she makes her husband his soup and sandwich because it gives him so much pleasure when she does.

THE THEME: *"The theme would have to be partnership.* We're partners in child rearing, where we've each carried large hunks of the load. We've been partners financially in trying to build what we have together. We've been partners as friends. Absolutely he's my best friend."

Now forty-six, Barbara is outspokenly satisfied with her life. There have been problems with one of the children and she wishes her husband were more patient with all of them. She also wishes he was not the kind of man who "thinks it's funny to put on wacky glasses and roll his eyes and make jokes."

AT FIFTEEN: "I think she would be pleased that things have worked out the way they have. A big surprise to a fifteen-year-old would be the way my husband's turned out. When I first met him, I thought he was a stuffed shirt. We'd gone out two or three times and he hadn't tried any hanky-panky, he hadn't even had a beer. But it's been just the opposite of what most people probably experience, where the guy comes with flowers and folderol until he wins his bride, and then can't remember her birthday. He's probably more attracted to me today than the day he married me. He was real scrawny when he was young, so when he filled out, he got to be the right size. When I was young, I might have said he's a nice enough guy, nothing special. But now he looks really good. He doesn't look fifty at all."

HOPE

Hope's mother, a biologist, was a somewhat rigid woman and her stepfather was, in Hope's words, "not very nice to me." It was from a loving grandmother and a successful, exuberant grandfather that the nurturing support in her early life came.

AS A GIRL: "I don't think I knew any women who weren't married. I liked to play house and play with dolls, and I just assumed I would grow up and have babies. But it never occurred to me that I wouldn't have a career. I would combine them the way my mother did, at least I knew it was possible. Black women have always worked, we haven't had any choice."

Hope married because she fell madly in love with her husband and, she says, "If I were single at this point I don't know that I would do it any differently. Even when casual sex wasn't dangerous, it's just not in my makeup. It would have to be someone I really cared about and I thought we'd really made a commitment to each other. I'm on the more conservative side of the border."

THE THEME: *"The theme of my marriage is push and pull.* I don't wish I was married to somebody else but sometimes I wish that he was not so demanding of my time and my energy, because it's draining. I think even though he loves children he would love for it just to be the two of us so he could have all of my attention. I would like him to respond to my need when I'm tired and falling apart or have a problem in the same way he did when we were dating—and not want me to be strong all the time."

Now forty-nine, Hope works hard. She seems to love her job as well as the time she spends with her children. But add to that a big, old house, community and professional meetings, and time for her marriage—it's a full plate.

AT FIFTEEN: "The young girl would say, 'Well, at least he's better than the boyfriend you grew up with.' I think she would see I have a husband who loves me, I don't have any question about that, and I love him. That's the important part and we can work the rest out. But I don't look forward to the children being grown. I'm a little worried because I get my sustenance from them. My husband and I have a lot to hold the relationship together but, when I'm exhausted or depressed, or just when I need some sustenance, I get it from the children, if it's no more than sitting in bed snuggling and reading. I don't know if a fifteen-year-old would understand all that."

RACHEL

Rachel is the daughter of cultured southerners who had a rich social life, worked and played together, and apparently gave priority to their own relationship.

AS A GIRL: "I assumed I'd have the sort of marriage my parents had. My parents, in fact, had a more modern marriage than I have. It would have seemed very lonely to me never to marry. So many things in my childhood revolved around things done as a family and things done as a couple. When I was a child, we sometimes played dressing up and getting married and talked about having children. But, as to the husband, he just wasn't in the picture. It wasn't until later on, when I was depressed and also afraid of supporting myself that I wanted the security of marrying someone who was going to be successful, who would make me feel emotionally and financially secure."

Rachel married two years out of college. That she was completely dependent on her husband for financial support, she believes, led to her complete responsibility for all the child care and household work. In recent years the economic balance has been shifting, and she also has been going about more on her own.

THE THEME: "*A lot of the time I feel like it's Friday night and I don't have a date.* Sometimes I do things that I don't particularly want to do because he wants me to and I try to have a good time. I want him to do the same for me. I want the partnership and companionship I saw in my parents' marriage—which I don't have."

Now forty-six, with her children going off to college, Rachel feels that her marriage is at a crossroads and that things will inevitably change, in ways she is not sure of.

AT FIFTEEN: "When I was young, it never occurred to me that you could be married and feel like you didn't have a date. Particularly if you were like me back then, too tall and skinny, with a big nose. That's not the marriage I would have wanted. If I were just starting out now, I'd be much more aware of what I needed."

SARA

Sara grew up in a comfortable and sophisticated home. She feels that it took her a long time to mature because, though her parents "idealized" her, they did not give her the skills she needed to make her way in an adult world.

AS A GIRL: "My parents had a turbulent marriage. There was love and joy, but there was also a lot of unhappiness; they were both, as individuals, unhappy. I'm a pleasure-loving person. I was very exuberant as a child and a teenager. For that reason, I just didn't see marriage as something I wanted."

Sara made her first marriage at twenty-nine, to a young man from the indigenous community she was then studying. She divorced after a few years and married her present middle-class American husband when she was thirty-seven.

THE THEME: *"I think fighting for fulfillment might be my theme, even in my marriage.* For my husband, after the loss and sadness of a bad divorce, he found a chance again; this marriage is the brass ring. But my quest has been to find someone who's worthy of me, that's been my narrative of myself that my parents imparted to me. I think there's still a sense of my not having quite lived up to my own expectations."

Sara is now thirty-eight, trying to get pregnant and to overcome the sexual difficulties in her marriage. Though she has an interesting career, she does not think it's "going anywhere" and focuses instead on the emotional content of her relationship with her husband and parents.

AT FIFTEEN: "The young girl would maybe be astonished at the older one's ability to have accomplished what she did. Even though it was such a lurching process, I have a husband I'm committed to and a career I enjoy. In a way, the kind of love that I have with my husband is very familiar—it's like I've never left home. The fifteen-year-old would have seen that but maybe with some regret because there's also this adolescent urge in me that I should've been a rock singer, or some United Nations official who'd go all over the world. I have a sense that I'm not necessarily where I would want to be."

GINGER

Ginger's father was an international banker and she grew up in Europe. Her parents' marriage was sometimes difficult but, she says, "they always hung in there."

AS A GIRL: "I never thought to myself when I was a young girl, I want a man with whom I can talk. I was much more affected by the image of the Prince Charming, very masculine, able to handle anything and everything, someone for me to lean on. I was a bookworm so a lot of it came from books, from the classics like *Jane Eyre*. I dreamed of Heathcliff, but I also had my mother as a model. I saw a lot of strength in her but also femininity."

At thirty-three Ginger married someone from a different religious background with whom she has had a marriage turbulent enough that the couple has sought counseling. She believes that her own strong personality is an important element in their difficulties.

THE THEME: *"We're a partnership, that's the theme, but I think I overstepped.* He feels bossed around. It has been in my court and that's what I'm trying to relinquish. I'm trying to go back to a more equal partnership."

Now thirty-seven, Ginger is getting ready to leave her high-profile, well-paying career and to trust her husband not to react to her new dependence on him by "playing mind games."

AT FIFTEEN: "I think I would have been surprised by how much fun it is, because he's a very fun person. I'm not sure that's what I expected. I like my marriage but it's not what I envisioned when I was young, in the sense that I probably was looking for a tall, dark, handsome answer to every problem I ever had, who also kept me titillated and excited forever. I don't have that and we do have problems, especially about sex, that I couldn't have imagined when I was fifteen."

MARIA

Maria's father drank, used drugs, and was abusive to her mother. Yet Maria says that her mother continually instructed her daughters that "if you want to hang on to a man, do what he wants, and be who he wants you to be. Do whatever you have to do to hang on to him."

AS A GIRL: "I thought about marriage only in passing. I had no idea, no picture; I could not imagine who I would marry, what they could possibly see in me. I thought it would be incredible if someone would even want to hold my hand or kiss me, that was just the most amazing thing to me. I thought more about having kids; that was easier to imagine than marriage, because of my parents. Not dreaming about marriage definitely had to do with them."

At twenty-two Maria married a man who, as she did, had a drinking problem. They both have stopped drinking and seem particularly happy, particularly appreciative of each other.

THE THEME: *"The theme is that marriage is work, but it's worth everything.* You really can't be selfish anymore. You have to listen even when you're tired, or you've heard it before, or you're not interested, or you're bored—you've got to be there. It's a small sacrifice, but it really works. My husband saved my life. I can't imagine being this happy in any other possible situation."

Now twenty-six and pregnant with her first child, Maria has a part-time job and is working on her bachelor's degree.

She hopes to become a therapist specializing in substance-abuse.

AT FIFTEEN: "I didn't expect anything. I still can't believe that I got even one-tenth of what I have. The fifteen-year-old was in a relationship with a guy who was hitting her. She would be very happy, very relieved, and very amazed that it would turn out just like the movies. I'm not portraying my husband as a saint. We both have very difficult aspects of our lives and personalities; but I never imagined I would have the marriage that I have."

AMY

Amy is the adopted daughter of parents who run a small, lucrative business together. When she was growing up, she and her girlfriends would play a game in which they pretended to be jaguars or cougars. Why? "They're very feminine and yet they're very powerful and I bet that's what did it for me."

AS A GIRL: "My parents have a very happy marriage, the happiest of practically anyone I know. Everyone else talks about how their parents don't get along but my parents are still cute. They still show affection and speak well of each other. My father is a very quiet, reserved person, so I was not exposed to the aggressive, domineering man when I grew up. I also was influenced even at a very young age by the women's movement. Even though I assumed I was going to get married, I never had fantasies that someone was going to take care of me. I was always going to take care of myself."

Twenty-five when she married, Amy had to push and shove until her husband acknowledged that he was as in love with her as she was with him. They are both scientists at important universities but Amy believes that she is headed for the more lucrative and prestigious career.

THE THEME: *"The theme of our marriage is that we're friends, but we have a lot of freedom too.* The other day we were both very tired and we fell asleep on our opposite wing chairs and it was just nice, knowing that our feet were touching on the stool in between. Sometimes I go away skiing for the weekend without him, because my husband's not all that into it. It's not a threat and it's not that I don't want him around. I would rather he be with me, but I can still go and have fun."

Amy is now twenty-eight, and though her marriage went through a stressful time when she was preoccupied with her weight, at this point the couple seems peacefully but vitally engaged.

AT FIFTEEN: "I think the fifteen-year-old would be pleased with it. After all, I married a feminist. I see marriages that are much worse than mine all the time, never ones that I think are better. Things might change, but it's hard for me now to imagine things changing enough that we would split up. Ever."

....

To which we can only reply, "Amen," a response that has the short punch of Rachel's marriage theme: "It's Friday night and I don't have a date." Miriam, whose ex-husband abused her from the first week of their marriage, said, "The theme of my marriage was Auschwitz." Erica, the widow with ten children, said, "We both had a really good sense of humor, so we could cope with this complicated life." Kay, whose husband made her put the bridal linens they needed back on the store shelves to assert who was boss, said, "He always, always put me down." And Joyce, with tears in her eyes, but smiling all the while, said quietly, "We dance so well together."

When the interview process was over, I tried playing the "theme game" with my childhood friend. Volunteering to begin with my own former marriage, without any thought I blurted out, "We married young and grew up differently." Her answer? "We both knew how to change." Perhaps it's a game we should all play *before* we marry. Perhaps asking "What should the theme of my marriage be?" would cut through the pink fog of daydreams that screens so many of us from a clear picture of the life we want.

INDEX

Abortion, 61, 89; pregnancy and marriage chosen instead of, 19, 20; regret over, 92

Abuse, disputes settled with, 167. *See also* Sexual abuse

Abusive father: physical abuse by, 98; pressure to marry due to, 17; sexual abuse from, 13, 78–79

Adolescent children: fathers and, 98, 100; parents quarreling over, 100

Adornment, sex and, 69–71

Advertisements, daydreams about marriage shaped by, 29–30

Affair(s): custody to husband having, 99; husbands having, 99, 157–58; women having, 157

Age: as pressure to marry, 14–15; too young at marriage, 181. *See also* Generational differences

AIDS, condoms and, 61

Alcoholic father: avoidance of marriage by daughter due to, 12–13, 14; nondaydreaming of marriage and, 32

Anti-models: family friends and relatives influencing expectations of marriage as, 4, 26–27; family influencing career as, 113; parents influencing financial expectations as, 131, 133

Appearance, sex and, 67–74

Baptism, religious differences and quarrels over, 101

Basinger, Jeanine, 115–16

Birth-control pill, sex and, 60–61

Body image, sex and, 67–74

Books: body image shaped by, 67; daydreams about marriage shaped by, 30; sexual expectations shaped by, 52; sexual revolution and, 62

Boston Women's Health Book Collective, 60

Brownmiller, Susan, 62

Calculators: career and, 109; happy first marriage and, 5, 32–34; qualities of husband and, 38–41

Career, 6, 108–29; children and, 15–16, 92, 94, 95, 96–97, 99, 117–20, 122–29; daydreams about, 6, 109–10, 114–16, 124; family expectations of, 111–13; gender prejudice and, 116–17; generational differences in attitudes toward, 108–9; happiness from, 125–29; husband/marriage and, 110–11, 115–16, 120–22, 123–24, 127, 128, 142; society's attitudes toward, 114–16. *See also* Money

Chance, choice of husband and, 49

Change, belief in, 40, 190

Childhood sexual abuse, by father, 13, 78–79

Children, 2, 7, 11, 88–107; adolescent, 98, 100; age of bearing, 15, 88–89; as better than any dream, 7, 89–93; career and,